OFFICIAL GUIDE TO THE
SMITHSONIAN
THIRD EDITION

SMITHSONIAN BOOKS

WASHINGTON AND NEW YORK

Library of Congress Cata-
loging-in-Publication Data
Smithsonian Institution.
Official guide to the Smith-
sonian. — 3rd ed.
    p. cm.
ISBN 978-1-58834-268-3

1. Smithsonian
Institution–Guidebooks.
2. Washington (D.C.)–Guidebooks. 3. New York (N.Y.)–
Guidebooks. I. Title.

Q11.S3S664 2009
917.5304'4—dc22
2009026696

Printed in China, not at
government expense

13 12 11 10 09   1 2 3 4 5

Guidebook Staff
Executive Editor:
Carolyn Gleason
Editor: Christina Wiginton
Production Editor:
Shalini Saxena
Designers: Jody Billert/
Design Literate, Inc., and
Amber Frid-Jimenez

The following are among
the many individuals who
provided invaluable assis-
tance in the preparation of
this edition: Laura Baptiste,
Rebecca Barker, Nancy
Bechtol, Bill Bloomer, Toni
Brady, Laura Brouse-Long,
Harold Closter, Joyce
Connolly, Tim Cronen, Linda
Deck, Dru Dowdy, Allison
Gallaway, Jane Gardner,
Margie Gibson, James
Gordon, Kathleen Hanser,
Valeska Hilbig, Jo Hinkel,
Mark Hirsch, Bob Hoage,
James Hobbins, Christine
Hoisington, Deborah
Horowitz, Elizabeth John-
son, Sarah King, Barbara
Kram, Sidney Lawrence,
Leonda Levchuk, Kathy
Lindeman, Patricia Lindsey,
Mary Ann Livingston,
Karl Ljungquist, Melinda
Machado, Carolyn Margolis,
Carolyn Martin, Kimberly
Mayfield, Joan Mentzer,
Helen M. Morrill, Dale Mott,
Catherine Perge, Nancy
Pope, Susan Post, Mary
Grace Potter, Elizabeth
Punsalan, Betsy Robinson,
David Romanowski,
Savannah Schroll, Jo Ann
Sims, Lou Stancari, Frances
Stevenson, Joseph Suarez,
Thomas Sweeney, Maureen
Turman, Michelle Urie,
Amy Wilkins, Emily Winetz,
Susan Yelavich.

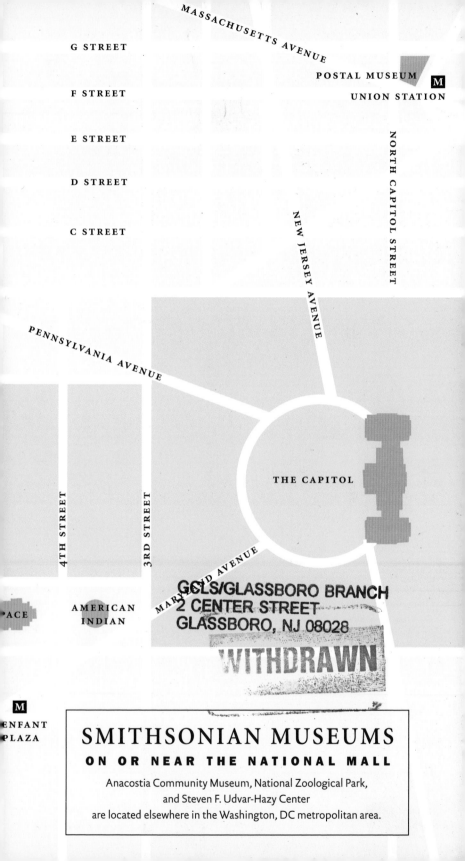

CONTENTS

WELCOME TO THE
SMITHSONIAN

Welcome to the Smithsonian! Through our 19 museums and galleries, National Zoo, and numerous research centers, we offer a wide variety of exciting, inspiring experiences for the whole family. Whether you're interested in art, science, history, or culture, there is something here for everyone. Your visit can continue long after you've gone because, increasingly, we are making our experts and collections accessible online. It is now easy and convenient for our conversation to continue.

For more than 163 years, the Smithsonian has remained true to its mission, "the increase and diffusion of knowledge," and currently maintains scholarly contacts or conducts research in nearly 90 countries around the world. The Smithsonian is involved in pressing issues of the day in science, education, and issues of national identity. It is a vast enterprise that encompasses – in addition to exhibition halls and art galleries – laboratories, observatories,

field stations, scientific expeditions, classrooms, performing arts events, publications, affiliate museums, the world's largest traveling exhibition service, a cable television channel, numerous Web sites and blogs, and much more.

The remarkable collections of the Smithsonian are the basis for research, exhibitions, and public programs in art, history, and science. Our collections include nearly 137 million artifacts, works of art, and scientific specimens. Among them are objects that speak to our nation's unique inquisitiveness, bold vision, creativity, and courage: Edison's light bulb and Morse's telegraph, the Wright flyer, the Apollo 11 command module *Columbia,* Lewis and Clark's compass, Colin Powell's Desert Storm uniform, Mark Twain's self-portrait, and Oscar the Grouch.

Through its creative staff and collections, the Smithsonian presents the astonishing record of American historical, cultural, and scientific achievement with a scope and depth no other institution in the world can match.

In the pages that follow, you'll find many treasures of the Institution pictured and described.

Through exciting exhibitions, *Smithsonian* magazine, the Smithsonian Channel, blogs, affiliate museums, lectures, and tours, the Smithsonian connects Americans to their heritage. You can contribute to America's ongoing story with your questions and comments, and we invite you to do so.

Enjoy your visit. Please come back often!

Opposite and preceding pages: Entrance to the Castle on the south side, from Independence Avenue and the Enid A. Haupt Garden. Overleaf: Located along the north side of the Arts and Industries Building is the Kathrine Dulin Folger Rose Garden.

Metrorail:
Smithsonian station.
For information about
the Smithsonian, call
202-633-1000 (voice)
or 202-633-5285 (TTY).
info@si.edu
smithsonian.org

Begin your
Smithsonian visit
at the Smithsonian
Information Center
in the Smithsonian
Institution Building
(the Castle) on
the National Mall,
open daily, except
December 25, from
8:30 A.M. to 5:30 P.M.

VISITING THE SMITHSONIAN IN WASHINGTON, DC

The Smithsonian Institution is a complex of 19 museums, the National Zoological Park, and numerous research facilities. Seventeen museums and the Zoo are located in the Washington, DC, area. The Cooper-Hewitt, National Design Museum and the National Museum of the American Indian, George Gustav Heye Center are in New York City.

Here is some basic information to help you plan your Smithsonian visit.

ADMISSION

Admission to all Washington Smithsonian museums, the National Zoo, and the National Museum of the American Indian, George Gustav Heye Center in New York is free.

Above: Edward Hopper (1882–1967), *Cape Cod Morning***, oil, 1950. Smithsonian American Art Museum. Below:** *Portrait of Yinti, Prince Xun, and Wife***, hanging scroll, ink and color on silk, China, Qing dynasty, 2nd half 18th century. Arthur M. Sackler Gallery.**

HOURS

Most Smithsonian museums are open daily, except December 25, from 10 A.M. to 5:30 P.M. (Check museum listings in this guide.) Extended summer hours are determined each year. The National Portrait Gallery and the Smithsonian American Art Museum—located in the Donald W. Reynolds Center for American Art and Portraiture—are open from 11:30 A.M. to 7 P.M. The National Zoo hours: April-October: grounds are open 6 A.M. to 8 P.M. and buildings from 10 A.M. to 6 P.M. (unless otherwise posted); November-March: grounds are open from 6 A.M. to 6 P.M. and buildings from 10 A.M. to 5 P.M. (unless otherwise posted).

HOW TO GET THERE

We recommend using public transportation, including taxis, when visiting Washington's attractions. Metrorail, Washington's subway system, and Metrobus link the downtown area with nearby communities in Maryland and Virginia. To locate the Metrorail station nearest the museum you wish to visit, see the individual museum entries in this guide. For more information, call Metro at 202-637-7000 (voice) or 202-638-3780 (TTY), or visit the Web site www.wmata.com.

To help navigate the largest museum complex in the world, the Circulator bus offers a quick and convenient service to Smithsonian museums. For more information on this inexpensive, hop-on/hop-off service, call 202-962-1423 or visit www.dccirculator.com.

The Smithsonian does not operate public parking facilities. Limited restricted street parking is available on and around the National Mall; posted times are enforced. Some commercial parking can be found in the area.

SMITHSONIAN INFORMATION CENTER

Open daily from 8:30 A.M. to 5:30 P.M. in the Castle, the Smithsonian Information Center offers visitors a multifaceted information and orientation program, with volunteer information specialists on duty to answer questions and give directions until 5 P.M. A free general brochure is available in various languages. Write: Smithsonian Information, Smithsonian Institution, SI Building, Room 153, MRC 010, P.O. Box 37012, Washington, DC 20013-7012. Call: 202-633-1000 (voice/tape); 202-633-5285 (TTY).

ACCESSIBILITY

For information on access to the Smithsonian for visitors with disabilities, see the Web site at accessible.si.edu.

ONLINE INFORMATION

A wealth of information about the Smithsonian and its resources is available online at www.smithsonian.org.

M. F. K. Fisher (1908–1992) by Ginny Stanford (b. 1950), acrylic on canvas, 1991. National Portrait Gallery. © Ginny Stanford.

PHOTOGRAPHY

Video cameras are permitted for personal use in most museums. Photography is permitted in permanent-collection exhibitions but is generally prohibited in special, temporary exhibitions. The use of flash attachments and tripods is prohibited in all buildings. Exceptions to these rules may occur in any exhibition or building. Ask at the information desk in the museum you are visiting for specific guidelines about photography.

PETS

With the exception of service animals, pets are not permitted in any of the museums or at the Zoo.

The Patent Office Building, the third oldest public building in the city, houses the Smithsonian American Art Museum and the National Portrait Gallery. It serves as an anchor to a thriving revitalized downtown where museums, restaurants, shops, and theater happily coexist.

SMOKING

Smoking is prohibited in all Smithsonian facilities.

WHERE TO EAT

Food service is available in the National Air and Space Museum on the National Mall and its Steven F. Udvar-Hazy Center in Chantilly, Virginia; the National Museum of American History, Kenneth E. Behring Center; the National Museum of Natural History; the National Museum of the American Indian; and the Donald W. Reynolds Center for American Art and Portraiture. The Castle Café offers light fare daily. The Zoo has a variety of fast-food services.

MUSEUM STORES

Located in most Smithsonian museums, the stores carry books, crafts, graphics, jewelry, reproductions, toys, and gifts that relate to the museums' collections.

SIGHTSEEING TOURS

Tourmobile, the only commercial sightseeing service federally authorized to operate on the National Mall, offers narrated tours with stops at Smithsonian museums, major memorials and monuments, government and historic buildings, and Arlington National Cemetery. Fees include reboarding options. Information is subject to change. Call 202-554-5100 (recording) or visit www.tourmobile.com.

The Chinese Moon Gate sculpture in the Enid A. Haupt Garden frames a view of the Freer Gallery of Art.

The National Mall has traditionally been the setting for large-scale events in the nation's capital.

THE NATIONAL MALL

A long, open, grassy stretch from the Capitol to the Washington Monument, the original National Mall was an important feature of Pierre L'Enfant's 1791 plan for the city of Washington. He envisioned it as a "vast esplanade" lined with grand residences. Before the Smithsonian Institution Building (the Castle) was built in the mid-19th century, however, the National Mall was used mainly for grazing and gardens. To the west, beyond the spot where the Washington Monument now stands, were tidal flats and marshes. After those areas were gradually filled, the National Mall was officially extended in the 20th century to the Lincoln Memorial.

In 1850, New York horticulturist Andrew Jackson Downing was commissioned to landscape the National

Mall. But his design, which called for curving carriage drives amid a grove of American evergreens, was only partly realized. By 1900, the National Mall had deteriorated. Its eyesores included a railroad station with sheds, tracks, and coal piles. Two years later, work was begun to implement L'Enfant's early concept. Over the years, much of his vision has become reality, with the National Mall now lined by rows of great museum buildings.

On the National Mall today, people jog, fly kites, toss Frisbees, or just stroll. Near the Castle, children ride on an old-fashioned carousel. For a time each summer, the colorful Smithsonian Folklife Festival fills the National Mall with traditional music and crafts. On the benches alongside the walkways, visitors rest while deciding which Smithsonian museum to explore next.

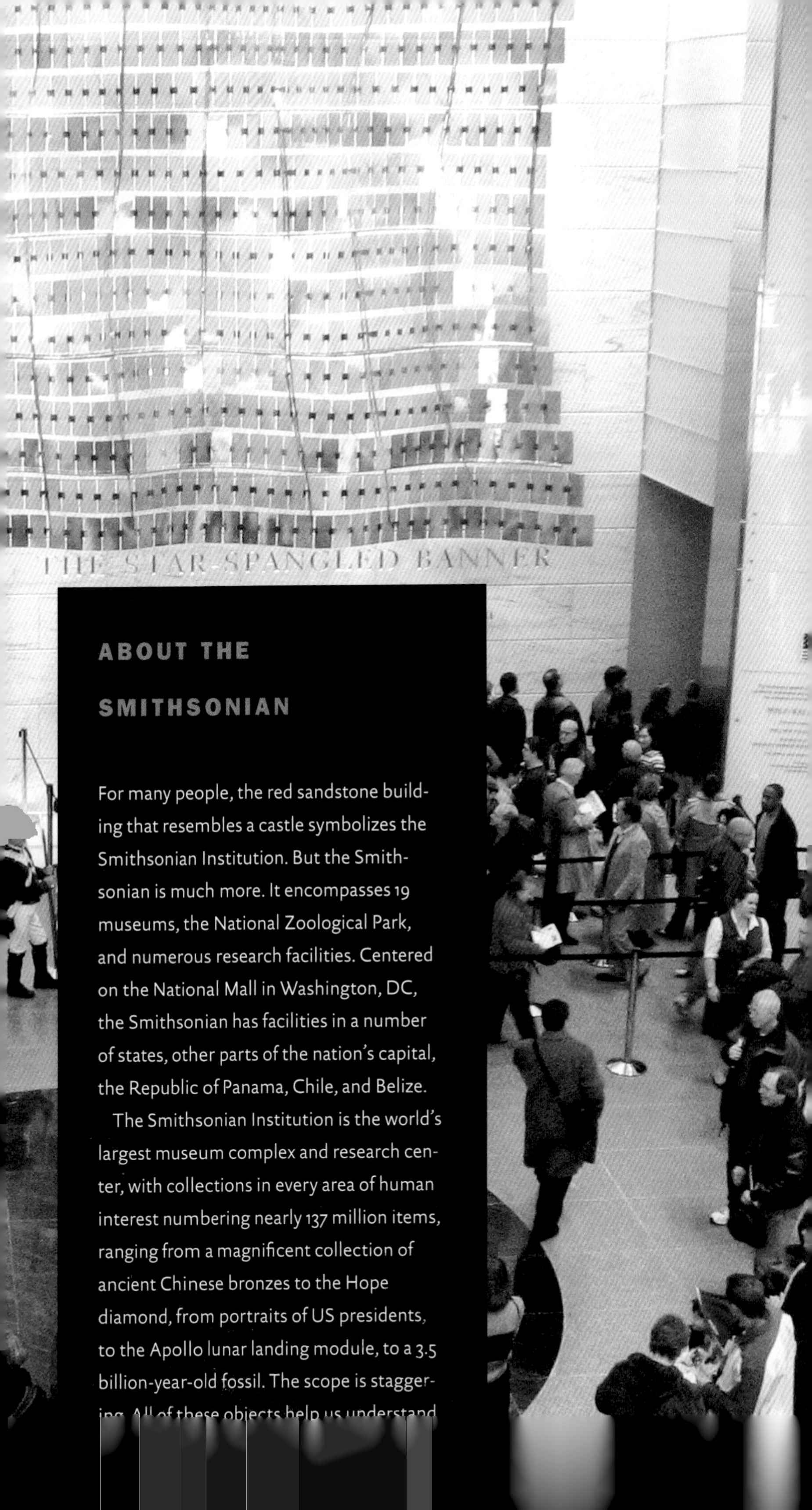

THE STAR-SPANGLED BANNER

ABOUT THE

SMITHSONIAN

For many people, the red sandstone building that resembles a castle symbolizes the
Smithsonian Institution. But the Smithsonian is much more. It encompasses 19
museums, the National Zoological Park,
and numerous research facilities. Centered
on the National Mall in Washington, DC,
the Smithsonian has facilities in a number
of states, other parts of the nation's capital,
the Republic of Panama, Chile, and Belize.

The Smithsonian Institution is the world's
largest museum complex and research center, with collections in every area of human
interest numbering nearly 137 million items,
ranging from a magnificent collection of
ancient Chinese bronzes to the Hope
diamond, from portraits of US presidents,
to the Apollo lunar landing module, to a 3.5
billion-year-old fossil. The scope is stagger-
ing. All of these objects help us understand

The design concept model for the National Museum of African American History and Culture submitted by Freelon Adjaye Bond / SmithGroup.

Preceding pages: After a two-year renovation, the National Museum of American History reopened to the public on November 21, 2008 with a Grand Reopening Festival. Historical characters, including George Washington, mingle with the public.

the past, consider the present, and preserve history for future generations.

Only a small part of the Smithsonian's collections are on display in the museums at any one time, but we are putting more of our experts and objects online. On expeditions to all parts of the world, Smithsonian researchers gather new facts and make discoveries in the fields of art, science, history, and culture.

NATIONAL MUSEUM OF AFRICAN AMERICAN HISTORY AND CULTURE

The National Museum of African American History and Culture was established in 2003 by an Act of Congress, making it the 19th Smithsonian Institution museum. It is the only national museum devoted exclusively to the documentation of African American life, art, history, and culture. The museum will be located on a five-acre site on the National Mall, adjacent to the Washington Monument and across the street from the Smithsonian's National Museum of American History. Though its facility isn't expected to be complete until 2015, the National Museum of African American History and Culture is already fulfilling its mission of tracing the impact African Americans have had on the United States. The museum's first exhibition "Let Your Motto Be Resistance: African American Portraits" is touring the country through 2011 as is its signature program "Save Our African American Treasures: A National Collections Initiative of Discovery and Preservation." For more information, call 202-633-4751 or visit the museum's Web site: nmaahc.si.edu.

A CENTER FOR LEARNING

The Smithsonian is deeply involved in public education for people of all ages. Visiting groups of schoolchildren are a common sight in the museums, and families come together here on weekend outings and summer vacations. Educators from the elementary school through the university level use the Smithsonian's resources, as do scholars pursuing advanced research. Through The Smithsonian Associates, adults and children enjoy classes, lectures, studio arts courses, and a variety of other educational activities.

The Smithsonian also offers an exciting schedule of "living exhibits." Performing-arts activities include music, theater, dance, film programs, and Discovery Theater performances for youngsters. The Smithsonian Latino Center (www.latino.si.edu) develops and supports public programs, research, and educational initiatives that highlight and further advance Latino contributions to art, science, and the humanities. The Smithsonian Asian Pacific American Program (www.apa.si.edu) traces and interprets the experiences of Asian Pacific Americans. The National Science Resources Center (www.nsrconline.org), an organization of the Smithsonian and the National Academies, works to improve the learning and teaching of science for all students in the United States and throughout the world.

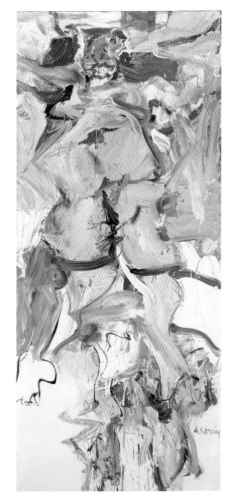

Willem de Kooning, (1904– 1997), *Woman, Sag Harbor*, 1964, oil and charcoal on wood. Hirshhorn Museum and Sculpture Garden.

Clockwise from top:
Conard and Jones Co.
1916 Floral Guide, *1916*;
Owen Jones *Examples*
of Chinese ornament:
selected from objects
in the South Kensington
Museum and other col-
lections, *1867*; John
F.C. Mullen *Official*
guide of the centennial
exposition of the Ohio
Valley and central
states: Cincinnati, O.,
U.S.A. 1888. Smithsonian
Institution
Libraries

SMITHSONIAN FOLKLIFE FESTIVAL

The popular Smithsonian Folklife Festival, a celebration of the nation's and the world's rich cultural heritage, brings musicians, craftspeople, cooks, and more to the National Mall each summer. Held outdoors for approximately two weeks every summer, the Festival educates a broad public about diverse cultural heritages and encourages tradition bearers by giving recognition to their artistry, knowledge, and wisdom.

SMITHSONIAN INSTITUTION LIBRARIES

This 20-branch library system boasts collections of 1.5 million volumes, in science, history, art, and technology, including more than 50,000 rare books and 10,000 exceptional manuscripts. Smithsonian Institution Libraries holdings also include a unique and distinguished collection of manufacturers' trade literature (430,000 pieces representing 30,000 companies) and World's Fair materials. All libraries may be visited by appointment. Digital exhibitions and digitized editions of rare books are on view at www.sil.si.edu. (For information about the Smithsonian Institution Libraries Exhibition Gallery, see the entry on the National Museum of American History, Kenneth E. Behring Center in this guide.)

NATIONAL OUTREACH

As a national institution, the Smithsonian takes cultural and educational programs to people across the country. The Smithsonian Associates provides educational and cultural programs through a variety of formats, including lectures, courses, and events on the National Mall and

across the country. Smithsonian Affiliations is a unique outreach program that shares Smithsonian collections, staff experts, researchers, and educational and programmatic resources with communities across the country. The Smithsonian Center for Education and Museum Studies offers educational experiences, services, and

Each spring, kite flyers from around the world take part in The Smithsonian Associates' Kite Festival on the National Mall.

products, and provides access to Smithsonian educational resources. The Smithsonian Institution Traveling Exhibition Service shares the wealth of Smithsonian collections and research with millions of people outside Washington, DC, through exhibitions about art, science, and history. (For more information on these national programs, see "Smithsonian Across America" at the back of this guide.) Smithsonian publications make available the expertise that its scholars assemble. *Smithsonian* and *Air & Space/Smithsonian* magazines publish lively articles on topics inspired by Smithsonian activities. Through the World Wide Web, home and school computer users have instant access to a rich resource with which to plan a visit, conduct research, find out about programs and exhibitions, and communicate with the Smithsonian.

RESEARCH AT THE SMITHSONIAN

The Smithsonian is a preeminent research center. Its research activities are known throughout the world for their benefit to the scholarly community and to the advancement of knowledge. Smithsonian scientists, historians, and art historians explore topics as diverse as global environmental concerns, the nature of the world's changing human and social systems, and the care and preservation of museum objects.

ARCHIVES OF AMERICAN ART

The Archives collects and preserves materials and makes available primary sources documenting the history of the visual arts in the United States. Headquartered in Washington, DC, the Archives also has a research center in New York City. For information, call 202-633-7940.

MUSEUM CONSERVATION INSTITUTE

The Museum Conservation Institute (MCI) is the center for specialized technical collections research and conservation for all Smithsonian museums and collections. MCI staff collaborates with and serves as a resource for in-depth studies of art, anthropological and historical objects, and natural history and biological materials using the most advanced analytical techniques to elucidate their provenance, composition, and cultural context. Their studies are also used to improve the Smithsonian's conservation and collections storage capabilities. Such studies require the latest instrumentation, analytical expertise, and knowledge of archaeology, art history, biology, chemistry, conservation, conservation science, geology, mechanical engineering, and interpretive abilities, all of which are available through MCI. For more information, call 301-238-1240 or visit MCI's Web site at www.si.edu/mci.

A Smithsonian Environmental Research Center technician measures the effects of exposure to increased concentrations of atmospheric carbon dioxide on accumulation of soil carbon in a brackish tidal marsh.

SMITHSONIAN CONSERVATION BIOLOGY INSTITUTE (FORMERLY SMITHSONIAN CONSERVATION AND RESEARCH CENTER), NATIONAL ZOOLOGICAL PARK

The 3,200-acre wooded area in the foothills of the Blue Ridge Mountains in Front Royal, Virginia, is a captive breeding and study center for rare and endangered animals. It is open to the public two days each year for the Autumn Conservation Festival. Parking fee determined annually.

SMITHSONIAN MARINE STATION AT FORT PIERCE

This research facility of the National Museum of Natural History serves as a field station that draws more than one hundred top scientists and students each year. Research focuses on the marine biodiversity and ecosystems of the Indian River Lagoon and the nearshore waters of Florida's east central coast. The station has also teamed with community partners

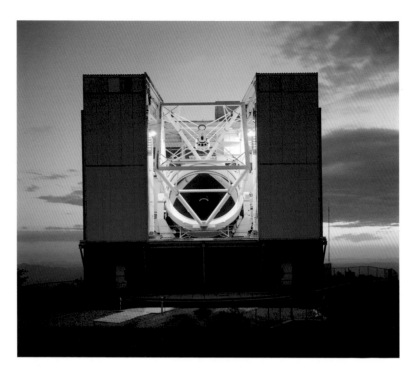

The Smithsonian Astro-physical Observatory's MMT Telescope glows against the Arizona sunset.

to create a marine science outreach center and public aquarium. For information, visit www.sms.si.edu.

SMITHSONIAN ASTROPHYSICAL OBSERVATORY

This research center is part of the Harvard-Smithsonian Center for Astrophysics (SAO) in Cambridge, Massachusetts. Smithsonian scientists are recognized leaders in theoretical astrophysics, ground-based gamma-ray astronomy, solar and stellar physics, extrasolar planets, the Milky Way and other galaxies, and the dynamics and evolution of the universe. SAO has observatories in Arizona, Hawaii, Chile, and Antarctica. The largest field facility is the Fred Lawrence Whipple Observatory on Mount Hopkins near Tucson, Arizona. SAO also manages the control center for NASA's Chandra X-Ray Observatory. For information regarding public programs, visit www.cfa. harvard.edu or call the Public Affairs Office in Cambridge at 617-495-7461 or the Whipple Observatory at 520-670-5707.

SMITHSONIAN ENVIRONMENTAL RESEARCH CENTER

Scientists and visiting researchers at the 3,000-acre site on the shores of the Chesapeake Bay, located seven miles south of Annapolis, Maryland, study land-water relationships and determine how they are affected by human disturbance. Staff conduct public education programs that disseminate the center's research and increase awareness of ecosystems, such as forests, wetlands, and estuaries. Distance Learning programs are available; call 301-238-1815 or visit www.serc.si.edu /education. For information about public programs, call 301-238-2737 or e-mail mcdonaldk@si.edu.

SMITHSONIAN TROPICAL RESEARCH INSTITUTE

Headquartered in Panama City, Panama, the Smithsonian Tropical Research Institute (STRI) furthers the understanding of tropical nature and its importance to human welfare, trains students to conduct research in the tropics, and promotes conservation by increasing public awareness of the beauty and importance of tropical ecosystems. For information, visit www.stri.org.

HISTORY OF THE SMITHSONIAN

The Smithsonian owes its origin to James Smithson, a British scientist who never visited the United States. Smithson named his nephew Henry James Hungerford as the beneficiary in his will. He stipulated that should Hungerford die without heirs (as he did in 1835), the entire Smithson fortune would go to this country. The purpose would be to found "at Washington, under the name of the Smithsonian Institution, an establishment for the increase and diffusion of knowledge."

The Smithsonian Tropical Research Institute studies the miniaturization of the brain in highly social individuals. Mark Seid focuses his research on how the behavioral repertoire of individual ants changes according to age and colony needs.

On July 1, 1836, Congress accepted Smithson's legacy and pledged the faith of the United States to the charitable trust. In 1838, after British courts had approved the bequest, the nation received Smithson's estate—bags of gold sovereigns, then the equivalent of more than a half-million dollars, a great fortune in those days. Eight years later, on August 10, 1846, President James K. Polk signed an Act of Congress establishing the Smithsonian Institution in its present form and providing for the administration of the Smithson trust, independent of the government itself, by a Board of Regents and Secretary of the Smithsonian. With the formal creation of the Smithsonian came a commitment to the work that continues today in research, museum, and library operation, and the dissemination of information in the fields of science, art, and history.

A statue of Joseph Henry, first Secretary of the Smithsonian, enjoys a prominent setting at the Castle's entrance on the National Mall.

Today, the Smithsonian is a national institution that receives a substantial appropriation from the federal government. Essential funding also comes from private sources, including the Smithson trust, other endowments, individuals, foundations, corporations, and revenues raised from such activities as membership programs, a mail-order catalogue, museum stores, and food services.

The chief executive officer of the Smithsonian is the Secretary. The Institution is governed by a Board of Regents, which by law is composed of the vice president of the United States, the chief justice of the United States, three members of the Senate, three members of the House of Representatives, and nine private citizens. The chief justice has traditionally served as chancellor of the Smithsonian.

Each museum has its own director and staff. The central administration of the Smithsonian is headquartered in the Castle building.

THE CASTLE

The Smithsonian Institution Building, popularly known as the Castle, was designed in medieval revival style (a 19th-century combination of late Romanesque and early Gothic motifs) by James Renwick Jr., architect of Grace Church and St. Patrick's Cathedral in New York and the Renwick Gallery of the Smithsonian American Art Museum in Washington.

A disastrous fire in 1865—just 10 years after the Castle was completed—caused extensive damage and the loss of valuable objects. Restoration of the building took two years. In the 1880s, much of the Castle was remodeled and enlarged.

The Castle originally housed the entire Smithsonian, which included a science museum, lecture hall, art gallery, research laboratories, administrative offices, and living quarters for the Secretary and his family. Today, administrative offices, the Smithsonian Information Center, and an exhibition titled "The Smithsonian Institution: America's Treasure Chest" are located here. The Smithsonian Information Center opens daily (except December 25) at 8:30 A.M.

The Smithsonian Institution Building, known as the Castle, was designed by architect James Renwick Jr. and completed in 1855.

Here, visitors can get questions answered by volunteer information specialists, pick up free brochures on the Smithsonian, and watch a film on the Smithsonian in the orientation theater.

ENID A. HAUPT GARDEN AND S. DILLON RIPLEY CENTER

Behind the Castle is a magnificent park-like garden named for its donor, philanthropist Enid Annenberg Haupt. Changing with the seasons, it features exquisite trees, shrubs, and flowers. In the center is a large 19th-century parterre. Pieces of Victorian garden furniture, some dating from the early days of the Castle and the Arts and Industries Building, are placed throughout the more than four acres of gardens. The garden is open from dawn until dusk daily except December 25.

Beneath the Haupt Garden is a three-level underground museum, research, and education complex that contains the Arthur M. Sackler Gallery, the National Museum of African Art, and the S. Dillon Ripley Center. The museums are accessible through aboveground entrance pavilions. Through a bronze-domed kiosk, visitors enter the Ripley Center, named for the Smithsonian's eighth Secretary. It currently houses the International Gallery with its changing exhibitions, workshops and classrooms for public programs, and a lecture hall. The Smithsonian Associates and the Contributing Membership Program have their offices in the Ripley Center.

OTHER SMITHSONIAN GARDENS

The Horticulture Services Division of the Smithsonian has designed and created many beautiful gardens around Smithsonian buildings on the National Mall. From mid-April through September (weather permitting), Smithsonian horticulturists lead 30- to 45-minute

The African crowned crane is one of the most spectacular birds in the National Zoo's collection. Opposite: The Enid A. Haupt Garden comprises three separate gardens, each reflecting the cultural influences celebrated in the adjacent architecture and museums. In the Fountain Garden, a *chadar* ("veil" of cascading water) delights the senses.

Top: The Mary Livingston Ripley Garden was created to honor the wife of the Smithsonian's eighth Secretary. Visitors meandering by its many curvilinear raised beds are treated to a profusion of seasonal plantings. Bottom: The Butterfly Habitat Garden.

tours. Check at any information desk for information about tours.

At the east end of the Castle, the Kathrine Dulin Folger Rose Garden features roses and other flowering plants that bloom year-round (seasonal tours). The Mary Livingston Ripley Garden, located between the Arts and Industries Building and the Hirshhorn Museum and Sculpture Garden, showcases hundreds of varieties of annual and perennial plants, unique hanging baskets, and unusual trees and shrubs. The Butterfly Habitat Garden on the east side of the National Museum of Natural History emphasizes the special interactions between plants and insects, which are described in interpretive signs.

The grounds surrounding the National Museum of the American Indian recall the natural landscape that existed prior to European contact, with more than 33,000 plants of approximately 150 species.

SMITHSONIAN SECRETARIES: 1846 TO TODAY

JOSEPH HENRY, a famous physical scientist and a pioneer and inventor in electricity, was founding Secretary from 1846 until his death in 1878. Henry set the Smithsonian's course with an emphasis on science. **SPENCER FULLERTON BAIRD**, a naturalist, served from 1878 until his death in 1887. Baird developed the early Smithsonian museums and promoted the accumulation of natural history specimens and collections of all kinds.

SAMUEL PIERPONT LANGLEY, whose particular interests were aeronautics, astrophysics, and astronomy, launched the Smithsonian in those directions during his years in office, from 1887 to 1906. **CHARLES DOOLITTLE WALCOTT**, a geologist and paleontologist, was Secretary from 1907 to 1927. During his administration, the National Museum of Natural History and the Freer Gallery of Art opened to the public, and the National Collection of Fine Arts (now the Smithsonian American Art Museum) became a separate museum of the Smithsonian.

CHARLES GREELEY ABBOT, Secretary from 1928 to 1944, was a specialist in solar radiation and solar power. He established a bureau to study the effect of light on plant and animal life, the precursor to the Smithsonian Environmental Research Center. **ALEXANDER WETMORE**, an ornithologist, succeeded Abbot in 1945. During his tenure, which ended in 1952, the National Air Museum (now the National Air and Space Museum) and the Canal Biological Area (now the Smithsonian Tropical Research Institute) became part of the Institution. **LEONARD CARMICHAEL**, a physiological psychologist and former Tufts University president, held office between 1953 and 1964. During those years, the National Museum of History and Technology (now the National Museum of American History, Behring Center) opened.

S. DILLON RIPLEY, biologist, ecologist, and authority on birds of East Asia, served from 1964 to 1984. Under his leadership, the Smithsonian expanded, adding the Hirshhorn Museum and Sculpture Garden, the National Museum of African Art the Renwick Gallery, and the Cooper-Hewitt Museum (now the Cooper-Hewitt, National Design Museum). The National Air and Space Museum moved to its present building, and construction began on the underground complex for the National Museum of African Art and the Arthur M. Sackler Gallery. Ripley also encouraged innovative ways of serving a wider public.

ROBERT McC. ADAMS, an anthropologist, archaeologist, and university administrator, served from 1984 to 1994. During his time as Secretary, the Smithsonian placed new emphasis on broader involvement of diverse cultural communities and focused on enhancing research support and education outreach. The National Museum of the American Indian was established as part of the Smithsonian during Adams's administration.

I. MICHAEL HEYMAN, a law professor and former chancellor of the University of California at Berkeley, was Secretary from 1994 to 1999. During his tenure, the Smithsonian began a program of reaching out to Americans who do not visit Washington, DC. Initiatives included a first-ever traveling exhibition of treasures for the Institution's 150th anniversary in 1996; a Smithsonian Web site; and the new Affiliations Program for the long-term loan of collections.

LAWRENCE M. SMALL served as Secretary from 2000 to 2007. During his tenure, the Smithsonian opened the National Air and Space Museum's Steven F. Udvar-Hazy Center, the new National Museum of the American Indian, and the Donald W. Reynolds Center for American Art and Portraiture. The National Museum of African American History and Culture was also established during this time.

G. WAYNE CLOUGH became the 12th Secretary of the Smithsonian in July of 2008. He is expanding the Smithsonian's global relevance and helping our nation shape its future through research, education, and scientific discovery. He has initiated long-range planning, and is making more of the collections accessible and available through a digitization effort. Secretary Clough has overseen several major openings, including the Sant Ocean Hall at the National Museum of Natural History and the reopening of the National Museum of American History.

ESPECIALLY FOR CHILDREN
THINGS TO SEE AND DO AT THE SMITHSONIAN

Before your visit, call Smithsonian Information at 202-633-1000 (voice/tape) or 202-633-5285 (TTY) and ask for "Ten Tips for Visiting the Smithsonian Museums with Children." Or check our Web site, www.smithsonian.org.

NATIONAL AIR AND SPACE MUSEUM

Both locations of the National Air and Space Museum offer a range of programs for families, children, and school groups. Stories, hands-on activities, science demonstrations, interactive displays, and special family-oriented days are available. Check at the museum's Welcome Center for a current events calendar and ask about events for the day. Older children especially enjoy the flight simulator rides and spectacular films shown on the five-story-high screens in the IMAX® Theaters. At the National Mall building, multimedia programs on astronomy and space in the Albert Einstein Planetarium are always popular. Simulators and shows have fees.

NATIONAL MUSEUM OF NATURAL HISTORY

Even after a tour of the museum's best-known treasures, there is still much, much more for families and children to do here.

• Hundreds of live butterflies flit from flower to flower, sip nectar, and roost inside the cocoon-like butterfly pavilion in *Partners in Evolution: Butterflies + Plants*. To purchase a ticket, visit www.butterflies.si.edu, call 202-633-4629 or 877-932-4629, or visit the pavilion box office.

• Next door at the O. Orkin Insect Zoo, children crawl through a termite mound, examine a real beehive, and hold insects. Staff members feed the tarantulas several times a day as an excited audience looks on.

• The Discovery Room helps visitors—especially the youngest ones—get excited about science. Touchable objects, kid-focused displays, and enthusiastic helpers encourage them to experiment, observe, and ask questions about what they see. Children must be accompanied by an adult.

• In the Samuel C. Johnson IMAX® Theater, visitors might take a fantastic journey through time or visit an exotic location in the 400-seat theater, which shows 2-D and 3-D films on its six-story screen. Admission fee. Tickets are available at the IMAX® box office. Visit www.si.edu/imax or call 202-633-4629 for more information.

NATIONAL MUSEUM OF AMERICAN HISTORY,
KENNETH E. BEHRING CENTER

Young visitors can charge their imagination at the "Spark!Lab"; explore "Invention at Play"; see the enchanting 23-room Dolls' House, view Kermit the Frog, and Dumbo, the Flying Elephant; and climb aboard a Chicago Transit Authority car in "America on the Move." Cart displays and touch stations will engage children in hands-on activities — such as cranking a cotton gin.

SPARK!LAB

Everybody can envision the "Eureka!" moment of invention, when the idea suddenly strikes and—BOOM—there's a new product ready to change the world.

"Spark!Lab" is a hands-on space for visitors of all ages that features games, science experiments, and inventors' notebooks, with a special section for kids under five.

INVENTION AT PLAY

What do the inventors of Post-it Notes, robotic ants, Kevlar, and the telephone have in common with children? Play! With its highly interactive and engaging activities, "Invention at Play" focuses on the playful creative skills and processes of inventors.

Please inquire about special activities and exhibitions at the Welcome Center on the second floor or the Information desk on the first floor, call 202-633-1000 or 202-357-1729 (TTY), or visit the museum's Web site at americanhistory.si.edu.

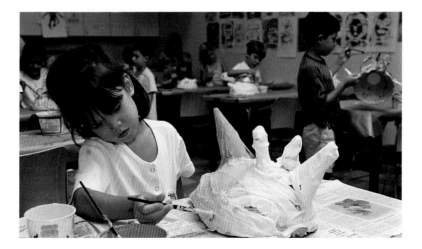

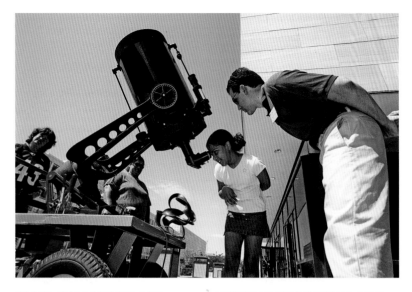

FREER GALLERY OF ART AND ARTHUR M. SACKLER GALLERY

Programs for young visitors include "ImaginAsia," which uses an adult-child self-guided art tour as inspiration for a project that children ages 8 to 14 may create with help from the education staff. Activity guides for some exhibitions also help family groups enjoy the gallery together.

NATIONAL MUSEUM OF AFRICAN ART

The arts and cultures of Africa are introduced to young audiences through workshops, storytelling, musical performances, and other activities. The popular "Let's Read About Africa" program, for children ages 5–10, introduces young audiences to current and classical children's literature about Africa. Programs for families are offered with many special exhibitions.

HIRSHHORN MUSEUM AND SCULPTURE GARDEN

Children accompanied by adults are invited to explore the Hirshhorn Museum and Sculpture Garden using our family guide and, on Fridays, to join interactive gallery talks designed to inspire the imagination. Children aged 6–12 and teenagers can register for special Saturday workshops created and led by artists that encourage participants to explore their individual creativity through gallery discussions and related art-making projects. These interactive programs may focus on a particular theme using work from the permanent collection or complement one of the museum's temporary exhibitions.

NATIONAL PORTRAIT GALLERY

The National Portrait Gallery includes innovative experiences planned for children and their families both in the galleries and in the NPG Education

Center, located on the first floor of the museum. For more information about upcoming programs, please visit the gallery's Web site at npg.si.edu or call 202-633-8500.

SMITHSONIAN AMERICAN ART MUSEUM

Kids of all ages will delight in finding art-works made from bottle caps, tin foil, or televisions throughout the galleries. The hands-on "Art a la Cart" activity, mobile carts located in the galleries, asks kids ages 7-12 to consider how artworks are created. Other free programs include Family Days, artist demonstrations, and musical performances. Developing scientists can watch conservators treat art treasures in the Lunder Conservation Center, and future curators can browse more than 3,300 objects in the Luce Foundation Center for American Art. Look for upcoming programs on the museum's Web site at AmericanArt.si.edu.

In addition, the Luce Foundation Center offers a daily self-guided scavenger hunt, and *Ghosts of a Chance,* a multi-media scavenger hunt presented monthly.

The museum offers a variety of online activities including *Picturing the 1930s,* a virtual 3-D movie theater; *Meet Me at Midnight,* an interactive online adventure; *¡del Corazón!,* which features interviews with Latino artists; and *Superhighway Scholars,* which includes a state history collage activity. These are available at americanart.si.edu/education/activities/online.

RENWICK GALLERY OF THE SMITHSONIAN AMERICAN ART MUSEUM

The Renwick Gallery offers a number of public programs and Family Days for children of all ages. Activities range from craft demonstrations and gallery talks to hands-on workshops with artists and musical performances. Look for upcoming programs on the museum's Web site, at www.AmericanArt.si.edu.

NATIONAL POSTAL MUSEUM

The museum is designed for a family audience, with state-of-the-art interactive displays, inviting exhibit design, and activities geared to adults and children. Try some of the museum's many audiovisual and interactive areas, including computer kiosks where you can personalize souvenir post-cards. Climb aboard a big-rig cab, a mud wagon, and a railway mail car. Discover the story of Owney, a stray dog who became the mascot for the Railway Mail Service. Participate in public programs offering a variety of hands-on activities and crafts, and check the museum's Web site for the current schedule of public programs.

ANACOSTIA COMMUNITY MUSEUM

Anacostia Community Museum exhibition tours are offered to schools throughout the year. Family activities at the museum include music, storytelling, festivals, and exhibition-related events and public programs. Also featured is The Museum Academy, a three-tiered project that includes an after-school program for elementary students, a career awareness program for middle school students, and an internship program for high school youth.

NATIONAL ZOO

Giant pandas, big cats, elephants, great apes, and reptiles are Zoo favorites for children of all ages. To see the pandas when they are most active, visit early in the day or late in the afternoon. Observe elephants being trained in the Elephant House or outside (weather permitting), or watch a seal and sea lion feeding and training demonstration.

In the Amazonia rainforest exhibition, explore specimens and artifacts in the biologist's field station. The Reptile Discovery Center features hands-on activities and the chance to see an endangered Komodo dragon, the world's largest lizard.

"How Do You Zoo?" in the Visitor Center and the Bird Resource Center in the Bird House are good places to discover more about the animals by exploring, looking, touching, and reading. Check for hours of operation at the Zoo's Visitor Center.

NATIONAL MUSEUM OF THE AMERICAN INDIAN

The National Museum of the American Indian in Washington, DC, offers a variety of engaging opportunities for families that will expand their knowledge of and appreciation for Native American cultures and traditions. Families can enjoy their visit to the museum by obtaining a free printed Family Guide at the Welcome Desk, participating in hands-on activities, attending regularly scheduled Family Days, taking a family or landscape tour, or seeing a film.

Throughout the year the museum offers a wide variety of craft demonstrations and performances that feature Native cultural arts—music, dance, drama, literature, and storytelling—in indoor and outdoor program venues. Be sure to stop by the Welcome Desk to learn what programs will be available on the day of your visit.

The museum's Resource Center has a handling collection of artifacts, children's reference and picture books, an electronic coloring book that can be e-mailed, and electronic postcards. Teachers can set up a time to bring their classes to the Resource Center for guided research by calling 202-633-6644.

The NMAI's George Gustav Heye Center in New York City hosts Native musicians, dancers, artists, and elders in presentations of their art and cultural heritage in informal programs that enable families to learn firsthand about the lifeways and world views of Native peoples. Kids can enjoy such diverse programs as theatrical presentations, hands-on workshops, storytelling programs, and annual events such as The Children's Festival and the Native Sounds Downtown concert series.

CAROUSEL ON THE MALL

For a perfect break from museums for adults and children, take a ride on the carousel on the National Mall near the Smithsonian Castle. The carousel operates daily, weather permitting; schedule varies seasonally. There is a small fee.

DISCOVERY THEATER

Located in the S. Dillon Ripley Center, this popular theater for young audiences approximately ages 2 to 16 presents live performances by storytellers, puppeteers, dancers, actors, and singers year-round. For show times, tickets, performance location, and reservations, call 202-633-8700 (recording/voice) Monday through Friday, or visit www.discoverytheater.org.

Above: The Bell X-1 *Glamorous Glennis* cockpit remains much the same as it was when Chuck Yeager first exceeded the speed of sound on October 14, 1947. Opposite top: Boeing F4B-40. Opposite bottom: *Continuum,* a cast bronze sculpture by Charles O. Perry, installed in front of the museum's Independence Avenue entrance.

Independence Avenue
at 6th Street, SW.
Mall entrance:
Jefferson Drive at
6th Street, SW.
Open daily from
10 A.M. to 5:30 P.M.
Closed December 25.
Metrorail: L'Enfant
Plaza station.
Steven F. Udvar-Hazy
Center
14390 Air and Space
Museum Parkway
Chantilly, VA,
off Rte. 28
Open daily from
10 A.M. to 5:30 P.M.
Closed December 25.
Parking available
for a fee.
Information:
202-633-1000
TTY: 202-357-1729
www.nasm.si.edu

NATIONAL AIR AND
SPACE MUSEUM

When visitors come to Washington, DC,
it's almost a sure bet that the National Air
and Space Museum is the first place they'll
go. People of all ages and backgrounds are
drawn by the museum's reputation as the
most visited museum in the world. Once
inside the building, their high expectations
are surpassed when they wander among
the museum's icons of flight and enjoy
other activities such as large-screen IMAX®
movies; flight simulators; planetarium
shows; guided tours; science demonstrations; and interactive devices.

Since its opening more than 30 years
ago, however, the National Air and Space
Museum's building on the National Mall
has been limited by size to displaying only
about 10 percent of the Smithsonian's aviation and space collection. Many rare and

historic artifacts were in storage and unavailable to the public.

In 2003, a much-anticipated companion facility, the Steven F. Udvar-Hazy Center, opened near Washington-Dulles International Airport, creating the largest air and space history complex in the world. Now the museum can exhibit nearly all of its collection, the only collection of its kind consisting almost exclusively of history's genuine icons of flight.

THE NATIONAL MALL BUILDING

The National Mall building presents the story of aeronautics and space flight in 23 galleries, each devoted to a specific subject or theme. Hundreds of historically significant aircraft, rockets, spacecraft, engines, propellers, scale models, pilot uniforms, space suits, awards, works of art, instruments, and pieces of flight equipment are on display.

A good place to start a visit is just inside the Mall entrance, where some of the major "firsts" in aviation and space history are featured.

GALLERY 100. Milestones of Flight
The central gallery of the Museum—in more ways than one.

GROUND LEVEL

MERCURY *FRIENDSHIP 7.* First U.S. piloted orbital flight, 1962; flown by astronaut John Glenn

GEMINI IV. First U.S. space walk, 1965

APOLLO 11 COMMAND MODULE *COLUMBIA.* First manned lunar landing mission, 1969

TOUCHABLE MOON ROCK. Collected from the lunar surface by Apollo 17 astronauts

The Ryan NYP *Spirit of St. Louis* in which Charles Lindbergh made his historic solo, nonstop, transatlantic flight from New York to Paris.

VIKING LANDER. Test vehicle for the first spacecraft to operate on the surface of Mars, 1976

BREITLING *ORBITER 3* GONDOLA. From the first balloon to fly nonstop around the world, 1999

GODDARD ROCKETS. Full-scale model of the world's first liquid propellant rocket, 1926, and a larger rocket, 1941

PERSHING-II (U.S.) AND SS-20 (USSR) MISSILES. Two disarmed missiles that represent the more than 2,600 nuclear intermediate-range ballistic missiles banned by the Intermediate Nuclear Forces Treaty of 1987

SUSPENDED FROM THE CEILING

SPACESHIPONE. First privately developed piloted vehicle to reach space, 2004

BELL X-1 *GLAMOROUS GLENNIS*. First airplane to fly faster than the speed of sound, piloted by Charles E. "Chuck" Yeager, 1947

RYAN NYP *SPIRIT OF ST. LOUIS*. Airplane in which Charles Lindbergh made the first nonstop solo transatlantic flight, 1927

BELL XP-59A AIRACOMET. First American turbojet aircraft, 1942

EXPLORER 1. Backup for the first U.S. satellite to orbit Earth, 1958

SPUTNIK 1. Soviet replica of the first artificial satellite to orbit Earth, 1957

PIONEER 10. Prototype for the first unmanned spacecraft to fly by Jupiter and Saturn and out of the solar system, launched in 1972

NORTH AMERICAN X-15. First piloted aircraft to exceed six times the speed of sound (4,534 miles per hour) and the first to explore the fringes of space, 1967

MARINER 2. Backup of the first interplanetary probe to study another planet (Venus), 1962

GALLERY 101. Museum Store

STAR TREK ENTERPRISE MODEL. Used in filming the television series

PITTS S-15 SPECIAL. Small aerobatic biplane designed by Curtis Pitts. It dominated the unlimited class in world-championship competition, 1960

SpaceShipOne, the first privately built and piloted vehicle to reach space, is now on display in the National Air and Space Museum's building on the National Mall.

43

The Lockheed F-104 Starfighter was nick-named "the missile with a man in it," since its long, thin fuselage and stubby wings resembled a missile more than a conventional aircraft. The F-104 was the first interceptor in the service of the United States to be able to fly at sustained speeds above Mach 2 (twice the speed of sound).

GALLERY 102. America by Air

The story of America's airline industry

DOUGLAS DC-3. A design milestone and perhaps the single most important aircraft in air transportation history, 1935. At 16,875 pounds, the heaviest airplane hanging from the museum's ceiling

FORD 5-AT TRI-MOTOR. Offered dependable, safe, and relatively comfortable service when introduced in 1928

PITCAIRN PA-5 MAILWING. Efficient, reliable airmail carrier, first flown in 1927

NORTHROP ALPHA. All-metal, cantilever-wing mono-plane with an enclosed passenger cabin, 1930

FAIRCHILD FC-2. First service aircraft of Pan-American-Grace Airways (Panagra), 1928

BOEING 247D. First modern airliner, 1934

DOUGLAS DC-7 (nose only). Visitors can walk through the cockpit of this 1953 airliner.

CURTISS JN-4D. Opened first scheduled airmail service, 1918

GALLERY 103.

Choose from a variety of ride simulations, including an excursion to the International Space Station or a sortie in various vintage aircraft. Or climb aboard one of 10 interactive flight simulators and try to become a jet combat "ace" as you pilot the simulator into 360-degree barrel rolls. Choose either pilot or gunner responsibilities.

GALLERY 104. Military Unmanned Aerial Vehicles (UAVs)

Unmanned vehicles for reconnaissance purposes and versions armed with weapons, ranging from the large and lethal to the tiny and portable.

GENERAL ATOMICS AERONAUTICAL SYSTEMS, INC.
MQ-1L PREDATOR. Predators have performed missions over Balkans, Afghanistan, and Iraq. The one hanging here flew 196 combat missions in Afghanistan.

BOEING X-45A JOINT UNMANNED COMBAT AIR SYSTEM (J-UCAS). Stealthy, swept-wing, and jet-powered, the first modern UAV designed specifically for combat strike missions

AEROVIRONMENT RQ-14A DRAGON EYE. By far the smallest aircraft here, this hand- or bungee-launched mini-UAV can provide reconnaissance and surveillance information to field commanders.

PIONEER UAV RQ-2A PIONEER. The RQ-2A provides field commanders with real-time reconnaissance, surveillance, target acquisition, and battle damage information.

GALLERY 105. Golden Age of Flight
Aviation between the two world wars

BEECH MODEL 17 STAGGERWING. Popular general aviation aircraft of the 1930s; the museum's Staggerwing dates from 1936

Above: The most successful airliner in history, the Douglas DC-3 dominated both commercial and military air transportation from its introduction in 1935 until after World War II. It was the first airplane that could make money by carrying only passengers. This one flew nearly 57,000 hours for Eastern Air Lines from 1937 to 1952.

WITTMAN CHIEF OSHKOSH *BUSTER*. From 1931 until its retirement in 1954, this midget air racer set records, including two wins in the Goodyear Trophy races.

CURTISS ROBIN J-1 DELUXE *OLE MISS*. Set endurance record of 27 days over Meridian, Mississippi, 1935

NORTHROP GAMMA 2B *POLAR STAR*. First flight across Antarctica, 1935

HUGHES H-1. Aircraft in which Howard Hughes set several speed records in the 1930s

GALLERY 106. Jet Aviation

The development of jet aviation and its related technology

MURAL BY KEITH FERRIS. A large-scale depiction of important jet aircraft, 1981

LOCKHEED XP-80 SHOOTING STAR *LULU BELL*. First operational U.S. jet fighter, 1944

MESSERSCHMITT ME 262 SCHWALBE (SWALLOW). World's first operational jet fighter, 1944

MCDONNELL FH-1 PHANTOM I. First U.S. jet to take off and land on an aircraft carrier, 1947

BELL 200L LONGRANGER II *SPIRIT OF TEXAS*. First helicopter to travel around the world, piloted by H. Ross Perot Jr. and J. Coburn, 1982

WHITTLE W.1.X. British experimental aircraft engine that became the foundation for the American jet engine industry when it came to the United States in October 1941

HEINKEL HES 3B TURBOJET. Replica of the engine that powered the Heinkel He 178 on the world's first flight of a turbojet-powered aircraft, 1939

PRATT & WHITNEY JT9D. Turbofan engine used in wide-body jet airliners

WILLIAMS WR19. World's smallest turbofan engine

GALLERY 107. Early Flight

Evoking the mood and excitement of the dawn of flight.

LILIENTHAL STANDARD GLIDER. A glider built in 1894 by Otto Lilienthal, an experimenter who inspired Wilbur and Orville Wright

The Messerschmitt Me 262A-1a, the world's first operational jet fighter, outperformed the best Allied fighters of World War II but entered combat too late to have much impact on the war. This rare example was one of many German aircraft captured and returned to the United States for testing. It scored 42 victories over Russian aircraft and 7 over American.

The Rutan *Voyager*, the first aircraft to fly non-stop around the world without refueling, is displayed in the south lobby. The *Global Flyer*, also designed by Burt Rutan, is on display at the Udvar-Hazy Center. It set several important aviation records: the first *solo* nonstop flight around the world; the nonstop distance record; and the closed-circuit distance record.

1909 WRIGHT MILITARY FLYER. World's first military aircraft

CURTISS D-III HEADLESS PUSHER. A favorite with U.S. exhibition pilots in 1911–12

ECKER FLYING BOAT. Earliest existing flying boat

BLÉRIOT XI. Louis Blériot made the first heavier-than-air flight across the English Channel in a similar aircraft on July 25, 1909

LANGLEY QUARTER-SCALE AERODROME. One of several powered, unpiloted aircraft built and flown by Samuel P. Langley. This one made two successful flights, in 1901 and 1903

LANGLEY AERODROME #5. First successful flight of a powered, unpiloted heavier-than-air craft of substantial size, 1896

AERONAUTICAL ENGINES. Some of the in-line, radial, and rotary engines that propelled airplanes from 1907 to 1914

GALLERY 108. Independence Avenue Lobby
The Rutan Voyager, *flanked by two murals*

THE RUTAN *VOYAGER*. First aircraft to fly around the world nonstop without refueling, 1986

THE SPACE MURAL: A COSMIC VIEW. Robert T. McCall's conception of the creation of the Universe, the triumph of lunar exploration, and an optimistic look at the future

EARTH FLIGHT ENVIRONMENT. Eric Sloane's dramatic depiction of the remarkable ocean of air that is our atmosphere

CONTINUUM. Bronze sculpture by Charles O. Perry, outside lobby entrance, 1976

GALLERY 109. How Things Fly

A hands-on experience that explores the science behind flight in Earth's atmosphere and space.

INTERACTIVE EXHIBITS. Dozens of mechanical and computer interactive devices demonstrate principles of flight related to air pressure and gravity, drag, thrust, lift, supersonic flight, aircraft and spacecraft control, and structures and materials.

The Lockheed U-2C, an important aerial mapping and surveillance craft since the 1950s, is a focal point of the "Looking at Earth" gallery.

LIVE DEMONSTRATIONS. Museum staff brings the science of flight alive with fun and engaging experiments and audience participation. Schedule posted daily at gallery entrance.

CESSNA 150. Learn how to maneuver an airplane; climb into the cockpit of a Cessna 150 and take the controls.

BOEING 787 CABIN SECTION. Discover what new materials and technology are being used in today's passenger jets.

BLENDED WING BODY (1/20 SCALE). Designed by NASA and Boeing, this 12' model was actually tested in the NASA Langley Research Center wind tunnel. It has a hybrid shape that resembles a flying wing but incorporates features of a conventional aircraft.

EXPLAINERS. High school and college-age staff members help explain the science behind flight with hands-on activities, historic objects, and engaging exhibits.

GALLERY 110. Looking at Earth
Development of technology for viewing Earth from balloons, aircraft, and spacecraft

DE HAVILLAND DH-4. A British-designed and American-built World War I military aircraft later used for airmail, mapping, and photography

LOCKHEED U-2C. The key U.S. reconnaissance aircraft of the Cold War era, with a flight suit worn by Francis Gary Powers and memorabilia from his imprisonment in the Soviet Union; and a surveillance camera dating from the late 1950s

EARTH OBSERVATION SATELLITES. Prototype of TIROS, the world's first weather satellite, 1960; engineering test model of an ITOS weather satellite, 1970s; half-scale model of a GOES geostationary satellite, and models of other satellites

LANDSAT IMAGE OF THE CHESAPEAKE BAY AREA. A 14-foot photomural, including Washington, DC, and Baltimore, Maryland

WHAT'S NEW. Developments in the science and technology of looking at Earth

This type of basket, held aloft by a hot-air balloon, was used in early aerial photography. The basket is in the "Looking at Earth" gallery.

GALLERY 111. Explore the Universe

How new astronomical tools—from Galileo's telescope in the early 1600s to the latest high-tech observatories on Earth and in space—have revolutionized our view of the Universe

EARLY ASTRONOMICAL TOOLS. Astrolabes, quadrants, and a celestial globe dating from 1090 to the 1600s, together with replicas of other instruments

20-FOOT TELESCOPE. The tube and mirror from the famous telescope used by William Herschel beginning in the 1700s to study the structure and nature of the Universe

OBSERVING CAGE AND CAMERA FROM THE 100-INCH TELESCOPE AT MT. WILSON OBSERVATORY IN SOUTHERN CALIFORNIA. Used by astronomer Edwin Hubble, whose discoveries changed our understanding of the nature and motion of galaxies in the early 20th century

PRIME FOCUS SPECTROGRAPH FROM THE 200-INCH TELESCOPE AT PALOMAR OBSERVATORY IN SOUTHERN CALIFORNIA. The most sensitive camera in the world mounted on the most powerful telescope in the world, this instrument helped astronomers in the latter half of the 20th century study the most distant galaxies yet seen.

HUBBLE SPACE TELESCOPE BACKUP MIRROR. This artifact, showing the honeycomb structure that supports

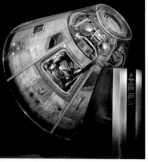

AT A GLANCE

The 1903 Wright Flyer, Charles Lindbergh's *Spirit of St. Louis,* John Glenn's *Friendship 7,* the Apollo 11 command module *Columbia,* and the walk-through Skylab orbital workshop are just a few of the attractions in this vast and exciting museum. Not to be missed are special IMAX® films projected on a screen five stories high and seven stories wide, providing a breathtaking cinematic experience.

Above: The Apollo 11 command module *Columbia* carried astronauts Neil Armstrong, Edwin "Buzz" Aldrin, and Michael Collins on their historic voyage to the Moon and back, July 16-24, 1969. Opposite: Lunar Module 2 is one of two remaining lunar landers built for the early Apollo missions.

the mirror surface, is nearly identical to the one currently in use on the Hubble.

CCDS AND OTHER LIGHT DETECTORS. Digital detectors from a variety of significant ground-, air-, and space-based instruments that were designed to explore every facet of the Universe

SPACE INSTRUMENTS. These are actual instruments returned from Hubble, plus full-scale engineering models and originals of the suite of instruments that mapped the big bang from the ground and from space.

GALLERY 112. Lunar Exploration Vehicles
Exploring the Moon

LUNAR MODULE. Backup of the Lunar Module that carried astronauts to the surface of the Moon in the late 1960s and early 1970s; Apollo space suit replicas

SURVEYOR LUNAR PROBE. Soft-landed on the Moon to study lunar soil composition and physical properties of the lunar surface, 1966–68

LUNAR ORBITER. Circled the Moon and mapped the entire lunar surface, 1966–67

RANGER LUNAR PROBE. Provided the first close-up photographs of the lunar surface, 1962–65

CLEMENTINE. Backup for 1994 robotic return to the Moon

GALLERY 113. Moving Beyond Earth
Explore the opportunities and challenges of human spaceflight on the shuttle, space station, and beyond.

LARGE SCALE MODEL OF SPACE SHUTTLE. Depicts the orbiter, external tank, solid rocket boosters, and mobile launch platform

FLIGHT SUITS. Worn by pioneering astronauts of the shuttle era

SPACE TOOLS. Used by astronauts to fix the Hubble Space Telescope

MODELS OF NEXT-GENERATION SPACECRAFT. Ares and Orion as they evolve

DISCOVER. What it takes to make a spacecraft reusable; what astronauts really do on the shuttle and

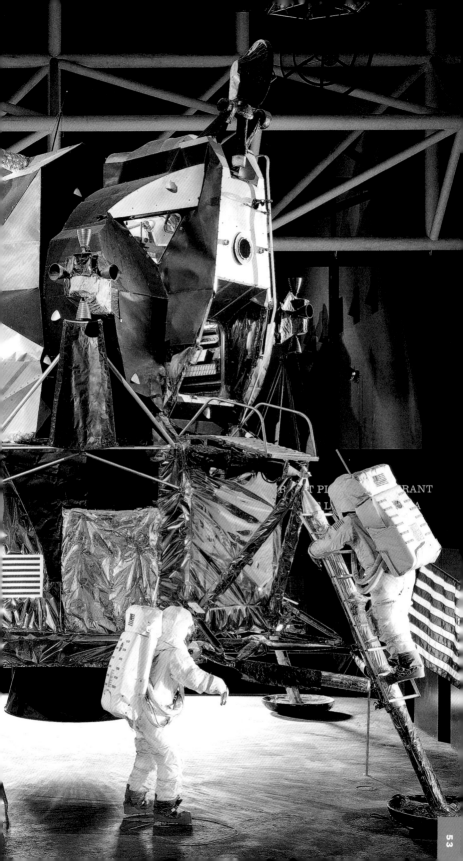

The "Space Race" gallery compares US and Soviet technology developed for manned lunar missions. At the left is a model of the US Saturn V rocket and an Apollo space suit worn on the Moon. At the right is a model of the Soviet N-1 rocket, which failed in test flights, and a Soviet Moon suit designed for a lunar landing mission that never occurred.

space station; and future plans for humans on the Moon and Mars

INTERACTIVE ACTIVITIES. Test your knowledge in the *SpaceFlight Academy* quiz game; see if there is *Space for You* and your talents on the Spaceflight Team; act as Flight Director to rescue a satellite in the interactive scenario *"Houston, we have a problem;"* build part of the space station in *Design It!*

GALLERY 114. Space Race

Tells the story of the United States' and the Soviet Union's competition in space and the race to the Moon

V-2. First operational long-range ballistic missile (German), 1944–45

AEROBEE. Major carrier of scientific instruments for probing the upper atmosphere, 1947–85

VIKING. U.S. Navy sounding rocket developed for scientific purposes, 1949–55

JUPITER-C AND VANGUARD BOOSTERS. First two U.S. satellite launch vehicles, 1958

SCOUT-D. Solid-propellant launch vehicle for scientific satellites, 1961–94

MINUTEMAN III. U.S. Air Force intercontinental ballistic missile, 1970 to the present

IVAN IVANOVICH, TEST FLIGHT MANNEQUIN. Mannequin sent into space by the Soviet space program a few weeks before the first human flight, March 1961

YURI GAGARIN FLIGHT SUIT. Flight suit worn during training by cosmonaut Gagarin, first person in space, April 12, 1961

JOHN GLENN SPACE SUIT. Worn by astronaut Glenn, the first American to orbit Earth, February 1962

SPACESUIT AND AIRLOCK FROM FIRST SPACEWALK. Cosmonaut Alexsei Leonov became the first human to "walk" in space, March 1965

APOLLO 15 LUNAR SUIT. Astronaut David Scott wore this suit on the Moon

CORONA CAMERA. This and similar U.S. cameras observed the Soviet Union from space

SKYLAB ORBITAL WORKSHOP. A walk-through, backup for the the first U.S. space station, 1973–74

APOLLO-SOYUZ TEST PROJECT. First human international space mission, 1975

HUBBLE SPACE TELESCOPE. Full-size engineering model of observatory put in orbit by Space Shuttle, 1990

The "Space Race" gallery contains many artifacts from the US and Soviet space programs. From left to right are the huge Skylab Orbital Workshop, a German V-2 missile, a cluster of rockets and missiles, and the Apollo-Soyuz Test Program display.

The history of ship-based flight is told in Sea-Air Operations, Gallery 203. Step aboard the simulated aircraft carrier **USS Smithsonian**, CVM-76, and visit the bridge, where you can observe aircraft catapulting off the bow.

GALLERY 115. Lockheed Martin IMAX® Theater
Large-format films are shown on a screen five stories high and seven stories wide. Admission fee. Schedule available at Welcome Center.

GALLERY 201. Albert Einstein Planetarium
Lectures on the night sky and multimedia programs on astronomy and space are presented in the domed theater. The planetarium projector simulates the nighttime sky and the motions of the Sun, Moon, and planets. Admission fee.

GALLERY 203. Sea-Air Operations
Aircraft carrier operations from 1911 to the present
CARRIER HANGAR DECK. Major aircraft from different periods in sea-air history
BOEING F4B-4. Biplane built for the U.S. Navy and Marine Corps
DOUGLAS SBD DAUNTLESS. Type of carrier-based dive bomber used during most of World War II
GRUMMAN FM-1 WILDCAT. Basic U.S. Navy and Marine Corps fighter aircraft at the start of World War II
DOUGLAS A-4C SKYHAWK. First-line naval attack aircraft of the 1950s and 1960s

CARRIER WAR IN THE PACIFIC. Depicts the six major aircraft-carrier battles in the Pacific during World War II

MODERN CARRIER AVIATION. Developments in carrier construction, operations, roles, and missions in the nuclear age

GALLERY 205. World War II Aviation

Fighter aircraft and related material from five countries

NORTH AMERICAN P-51D MUSTANG. An outstanding fighter airplane, used in every theater of the war

MITSUBISHI A6M5 ZERO FIGHTER. With excellent maneuverability and range, used throughout the war by the Japanese navy

MARTIN B-26 *FLAK BAIT* (NOSE SECTION). Flew more missions than any other U.S. bomber in Europe

SUPERMARINE SPITFIRE MARK VII. A later version of the legendary British fighter that helped defeat the Germans in the Battle of Britain

MESSERSCHMITT BF 109 *GUSTAV*. Principal Luftwaffe fighter and the major opponent of Spitfires, Mustangs, and U.S. bombers

MACCHI C.202 FOLGORE. Most successful Italian fighter to see extensive service in the African campaign and in Italy and the Soviet Union

MURAL. *Fortresses under Fire,* by Keith Ferris, 1976

The North American P-51D Mustang escorted high-altitude Allied bombers deep into Europe.

The Grumman FM-1 Wildcat was the Navy's main carrier fighter for the first two years of World War II. This version has a mechanism that allows the wings to fold back against the fuselage for a compact fit on the flight deck.

GALLERY 206. Legend, Memory, and the Great War in the Air

The emergence of air power in World War I

PFALZ D.XII. German fighter aircraft used in Hollywood films about aviation in World War I

VOISIN VIII. Early type of night bomber, 1915

SPAD XIII *SMITH IV*. French fighter aircraft flown by U.S. ace Ray Brooks of the 22nd Aero Pursuit Squadron

FOKKER D.VII. Considered the best German fighter aircraft of World War I

ALBATROS D.VA. German fighter aircraft that flew on all fronts during World War I

SOPWITH SNIPE. British aircraft considered to be one of the best all-around single-seat fighters, although it became operational only late in the war

GERMAN FACTORY SCENE. World War I mass-production techniques, with original equipment

HOLLYWOOD FILMS PORTRAYING A ROMANTIC IMAGE OF THE "KNIGHTS OF THE AIR."

Outside Gallery 206.

GOSSAMER CONDOR. First successful human-powered aircraft, 1977.

GALLERY 207. Exploring the Planets

History and achievements of planetary exploration, both Earth-based and by spacecraft

VOYAGER. Full-scale replica of the spacecraft that explored Jupiter, Saturn, Uranus, and Neptune in the 1970s and 1980s

A PIECE OF MARS. Meteorite collected in Antarctica that came from Mars

SURVEYOR 3 TELEVISION CAMERA. Retrieved from the surface of the Moon by the Apollo 12 astronauts

MESSENGER VIEWS OF MERCURY. Images of portions of the planet never seen by any previous spacecraft

WHAT'S NEW. Current planetary exploration

SPIRIT AND OPPORTUNITY. Mock-up of the rovers that landed on Mars in 2004

A full-scale model of a Mars Exploration Rover stands in the "Exploring the Planets" gallery.

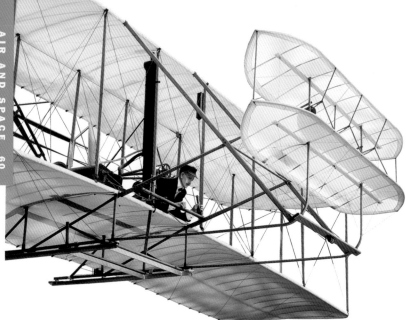

The 1903 Wright Flyer is the centerpiece of "The Wright Brothers and The Invention of the Aerial Age" gallery.

GALLERY 208. Barron Hilton Pioneers of Flight
Famous "firsts" and record setters

LOCKHEED SIRIUS *TINGMISSARTOQ*. Flown by Charles and Anne Lindbergh on airline route-mapping flights, 1930s

LOCKHEED 5B VEGA. First solo flight across the Atlantic by a woman, by Amelia Earhart, 1932

FOKKER T-2. First nonstop U.S. transcontinental flight, 1923

PIPER J-2 CUB. A stable and economical 1937 Cub light aircraft that made flying easy to learn and afford. This Piper J-2 is the first Cub built under the Piper name. Formerly known as the Taylor Cub, the J-2 model was soon modified into the world-famous Piper J-3 Cub.

"HOOPSKIRT," LIQUID FUEL ROCKET. A 1928 invention of famed rocketry pioneer R.H. Goddard.

INTERACTIVE ACTIVITIES. Hands-on elements for all ages, including pre-school children, throughout the gallery

BUD LIGHT SPIRIT OF FREEDOM GONDOLA. First solo flight around the world in a balloon by Steve Fossett, 2002

HAWTHORNE C. GREY BALLOON BASKET AND EQUIPMENT. Ushered in the era of stratospheric balloon flights, 1927

DOUGLAS WORLD CRUISER *CHICAGO*. First around-the-world flight, 1924

***EXPLORER II* GONDOLA.** This cabin and its balloon rose to a height never before achieved and made valuable scientific observations, 1935

BLACK WINGS: THE AMERICAN BLACK IN AVIATION. Exhibit chronicles the struggle of African Americans to earn a place in aeronautics and space flight in the United States

GALLERY 209. The Wright Brothers & The Invention of the Aerial Age
The story of how Wilbur and Orville Wright invented the airplane

1903 WRIGHT FLYER. The first heavier-than-air, powered aircraft to make a sustained, controlled flight with a pilot aboard

LETTER TO THE SMITHSONIAN. Read what Wilbur Wright wrote in this copy of an 1899 letter to the Smithsonian asking for information about aeronautics.

STOPWATCH. The Wrights used this stopwatch to time their first flights.

ST. CLAIR BICYCLE. One of only five bicycles manufactured by the Wright brothers known to exist today

ORIGINAL WIND TUNNEL INSTRUMENT. The lift balance with which the Wrights performed their pioneering wind tunnel research

ORIGINAL FABRIC AND PROPELLER. Both were on the Wright Flyer when it flew at Kitty Hawk in 1903.

HANDS-ON MECHANISMS. Learn about wing warping and other pioneering Wright brothers inventions.

FIRST FLIGHT SIMULATIONS. Watch video re-enactments of the first four flights of the 1903 Wright Flyer.

In 1932, Amelia Earhart flew this Lockheed 5B Vega solo across the Atlantic and nonstop across the United States.

Five huge F-1 rocket engines were needed to lift the 30-story-tall Saturn V rocket.

GALLERY 210. Apollo to the Moon

Triumph of human space flight in the 1960s and early 1970s, from Project Mercury through the Apollo Moon landings

F-1 ENGINE. Full-size, with cutaway of first-stage rocket engine used on the Saturn V rocket

SPACE TOOLS AND EQUIPMENT. Used to train for the Apollo missions

LUNAR SCENES. Showing the Lunar Rover and equipment deployed on the lunar surface

LUNAR ROVER. The type of vehicle that astronauts drove on the moon

SATURN BOOSTERS. Models of Saturn IB and Saturn V rockets

LUNAR SAMPLES. Four types of lunar soil and rocks

SPACE FOOD. How astronauts' and cosmonauts' food has changed

SPACE SUITS. Worn on the Moon by Apollo Astronauts

GALLERY 211. Flight
in the Arts
Rotating Exhibits
GALLERY 213. Beyond
the Limits: Flight Enters
the Computer Age
*How computers are used
in aerospace design and
operations*

X-29 (FULL-SCALE MODEL).
Forward-swept-wing airplane

CRAY-1 SUPERCOMPUTER. Once
the world's fastest computer

INTERACTIVE COMPUTERS. Visi-
tors can try out computer-aided design, flight simula-
tion, airline scheduling, and flight testing.

HIMAT. Robotic airplane that pioneered the use of fly-
by-wire technology, in which a computer, not the pilot,
controls the aircraft

MINUTEMAN III ICBM GUIDANCE AND CONTROL SYSTEM.
The brain of the Minuteman missile, the standard U.S.
land-based intercontinental ballistic missile

MOTOROLA IRIDIUM SATELLITE. Flight backup craft for
the world's first global, satellite-based telephone net-
work, 1998

GLOBAL POSITIONING SATELLITE (1/4-SCALE MODEL).
Space-based constellation of satellites used for precise
navigation and position location

EARTH TODAY. A DIGITAL VIEW OF OUR PLANET. See
an up-to-date picture of conditions on our planet in
close to real time.

Above: Using a rover like
this one, Apollo 17 astronauts spent a record 22
hours exploring the lunar
surface and collecting
rock and soil samples.
Below: *Mural Master
Study: Horizontal* by
Robert T. McCall, 1975,
acrylic on canvas, 58 x
229 cm (23 x 90 in.).

The Steven F. Udvar-Hazy Center is a magnificent example of architecture, as seen here at sunset.

STEVEN F. UDVAR-HAZY CENTER

The National Air and Space Museum's location in Chantilly, Virginia offers a unique museum experience. The 21st century building design is in itself an amazing sight, dominated by a 164-foot-high observation tower and the spherical IMAX® theater. Inside, artifacts are displayed in a massive open setting, organized in thematic groupings. Adjacent to the enormous aircraft and spacecraft—many too large to be displayed in the National Mall building—free-standing exhibit stations encourage visitors to explore the artifacts' historic context through text and images.

The ten-story Boeing Aviation Hangar contains aircraft suspended on two levels from the building's huge trusses, with larger aircraft on the floor. The suspended vehicles have been hung to replicate their typical flight maneuvers: an aerobatic airplane hot-dogging upside down, a World War II fighter angling for a victory, and a small two-seater flying level. Walkways rising four stories above the floor provide nose-to-nose views of aircraft in suspended flight.

The James S. McDonnell Space Hangar is dominated by the dramatically lit Space Shuttle *Enterprise*, around which hundreds of other space artifacts are

arranged. A free-floating astronaut appears to perform extravehicular activity above, and oddly shaped satellites and rockets dot the overhead space. The hangar features two elevated overlooks that allow visitors to study suspended artifacts up close and get a view of the entire hangar.

The Donald D. Engen Observation Tower contains interactive Flight Control displays and gives visitors a great view of aircraft taking off and landing at the adjacent Washington-Dulles International Airport.

Outside the Udvar-Hazy Center, the Wall of Honor leads from the parking lot to the building entrance. Panels evocative of aircraft wing foils are engraved with the names of those who have contributed to our nation's aviation and space exploration heritage.

Above: The James S. McDonnell Space Hangar is 80 feet high, 262 feet long, and 180 feet wide. Below: The National Aviation and Space Exploration Wall of Honor on the walkway leading to the Udvar-Hazy Center honors those who have contributed to our nation's aviation and space exploration.

Nearby stands the polished steel sculpture, *Ascent*, by local artist John Safer.

More than 200 aircraft and 135 large space artifacts will ultimately be on display. The artifacts listed here are only a sample of those currently on view.

The Boeing Aviation Hangar is organized into eleven sections.

PRE-1920 AVIATION

CAUDRON G.4. Used for reconnaissance, as a bomber, and as a trainer. The Museum's G.4 is one of only two that still exist.

NIEUPORT 28. America's first fighter airplane, the Nieuport was a French design flown by U.S. pilots in World War I.

BUSINESS AVIATION

LEARJET 23. The Model 23s were the founding products of the original Lear Jet Corporation and pioneers in the field of business and personal jet aviation.

SPORT AVIATION

ARLINGTON SISU 1A. The first motorless aircraft to fly beyond 1,000 km (620 miles) during a single flight in 1964.

The Caudron G.4 on display at the Udvar-Hazy Center is one of only two that still exist.

VERTICAL FLIGHT

AUTOGIRO COMPANY OF AMERICA

AC-35. In 1935, this "roadable" gyro-plane was a model for a suburban commuter aircraft. With folding blades and a powered drive wheel, it could do 25 mph on city streets and 90 mph in the air.

BELL H-13J. In 1957, this aircraft became the first presidential heli-copter. Its primary role was to evacuate the president in case of nuclear attack.

BELL XV-15 TILT ROTOR RESEARCH AIRCRAFT. First flown in 1977, the XV-15 was the first successful tilt-rotor aircraft. It could hover as a helicopter, but by converting to an airplane, it had much greater speed and range than was possible with a helicopter.

VOUGHT-SIKORSKY XR-4C. The culmination of Igor I. Sikorsky's attempts to create a practical helicopter, the XR-4 (1942) was the prototype for the world's first mass-produced helicopter. Its success sold the government on the military value of the helicopter and led to large-scale introduction of more advanced rotorcraft.

GENERAL AVIATION

PIPER J-3 CUB. Such an easy-to-fly, inexpensive airplane that thousands of private pilots, including many in the Civilian Pilot Training Program prior to World War II, learned to fly in it.

Above, front to back: The Bell Model 30 Ship 1A "Genevieve," Bell Model 47B, and Bell H-13J helicopters are now on display at the Udvar-Hazy Center. The Bell H-13J was the first helicopter to carry a United States president. Below: The experimental XV-15 tilt rotor was donated by NASA and the U.S. Army, and is featured in the Museum's peerless vertical flight collection at the Udvar-Hazy Center.

MONOCOUPE 110 SPECIAL *LITTLE BUTCH*. Woody Edmondson, air show pilot and aerobatic champion, thrilled air show crowds with his Monocoupe 110 Special throughout the late 1940s.

LOCKHEED 5C VEGA *WINNIE MAE*. A special Lockheed Model 5C Vega flown by famed aviator Wiley Post, the Vega completed two around-the-world record flights and a series of special high-altitude substratospheric research flights.

COMMERCIAL AVIATION

BOEING 307 STRATOLINER. The first airliner to have a pressurized fuselage. The museum's *Clipper Flying Cloud*, flown by Pan American Airways, is the only surviving Stratoliner.

CONCORDE. The first supersonic airliner to enter scheduled service, the Concorde flew for 27 years before Air France retired its fleet in May 2003. The museum's Concorde was the first in the Air France fleet.

BOEING 367-80. The "Dash 80" was the original prototype for the Boeing 707, America's first jetliner and the airplane that opened the world to faster, less-expensive air travel.

WORLD WAR II AVIATION

BOEING B-29 *ENOLA GAY*. Dropped the first atomic bomb used in combat on Hiroshima, Japan, on August 6, 1945.

CURTISS P-40E WARHAWK. One of the best known U.S. fighters of World War II. The Warhawk's greatest fame was achieved with the Flying Tigers, whose P-40s wore a shark-mouth paint scheme.

Above: Visitors to the Udvar-Hazy Center can see the Monocoupe 110 Special "Little Butch" hanging from ten-story-high trusses.
Below: The B-29 *Enola Gay* has been reassembled after 43 years and is on display in the Udvar-Hazy Center's World War II section.

CHANCE-VOUGHT F4U-1D CORSAIR. The F4U Corsair, the distinctive bent-wing fighter-bomber, acquired a unique reputation in military aviation as a fast and versatile aircraft. This airplane was both a land-based and carrier-based fighter, and established its distinguished

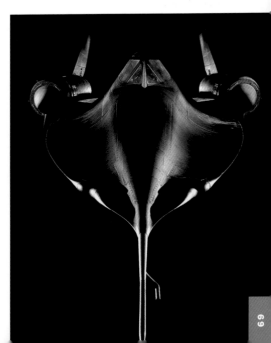

combat record in both World War II and Korea.

GRUMMAN F6F-3 HELLCAT. In 1943 Grumman introduced the Hellcat, one of the war's most potent fighter aircraft. American pilots now had an aircraft that was faster and almost as maneuverable as their Japanese opponents.

LOCKHEED P-38J LIGHTNING. The unique, twin-boom, twin-engine P-38 Lightning was one of the most versatile fighters of World War II. P-38s downed more aircraft in the Pacific than any other airplane.

AICHI M6A1 SEIRAN (*CLEAR SKY STORM*). The only surviving example in the world of a Japanese bomber that could operate exclusively from a submarine.

COLD WAR AVIATION

LOCKHEED SR-71 BLACKBIRD. The fastest, highest flying operational jet-powered aircraft ever built. On its final flight, the National Air and Space Museum's Blackbird set a transcontinental speed record when it flew from the West Coast to the East Coast in 64 minutes and 20 seconds.

MCDONNELL F-4S PHANTOM II. One of the most versatile military aircraft ever built, flown by the U.S. Air Force, Marine Corps, and Navy.

Above: The Air France Concorde F-BVFA, the oldest of the Air France supersonic fleet, is on display in the Commercial Aviation section. Below: The Blackbird's performance and operational achievements placed it at the pinnacle of aviation technology developments during the Cold War.

In addition to its high performance, the F-86A Sabre had excellent handling characteristics and was well liked by its pilots.

KOREA AND VIETNAM

NORTH AMERICAN F-86A SABRE. High above the Yalu River area of Korea, the F-86 Sabre joined the ranks of the great fighter aircraft. American pilots flying the Sabre established a significant victory ratio over enemy MiG-15s.

BELL UH-1H IROQUOIS (HUEY). What the jeep was to Americans during World War II, so was the Huey to those who fought in Vietnam. People knew it not just on sight but by the sound of the unmistakable whop-whop-whop of the main rotor blade.

REPUBLIC F-105 THUNDERCHIEF. Designed as a single-seat, fighter-bomber capable of carrying nuclear weapons or heavy bomb loads at supersonic speeds.

MODERN MILITARY AVIATION

LOCKHEED MARTIN JOINT STRIKE FIGHTER. A stealthy, multi-role fighter with many test records to its credit, including first to achieve a short takeoff, level supersonic dash, and vertical landing in a single flight.

AIRCRAFT ENGINES

A collection of aircraft engines is on display at ground level at the northeast end.

SMALL ARTIFACTS

Hundreds of artifacts and artifact collections, including aerial cameras, awards and insignias, machine guns, aircraft models, popular culture items, and pilot uniforms are displayed in glass cases.

The James S. McDonnell Space Hangar is organized into four categories:

ROCKETRY AND MISSILES

GODDARD 1935 A-SERIES ROCKET. One of several built by Dr. Robert H. Goddard as the "A-Series" between September 1934 and October 1935, this rocket used a pressurized nitrogen gas, rather than pumps, to feed gasoline fuel and liquid oxygen oxidizer to the engine, and gyro-controlled vanes located in the rocket exhaust provided stability.

CORPORAL MISSILE. Essentially a vertically fired artillery round. The first successful Corporal was fired on May 22, 1947, and the missile played an important part in the early Cold War.

REDSTONE MISSILE. The United States' first operational ballistic missile played a major role in the early U.S. space program.

PEGASUS. A three-stage rocket used by commercial, government, and international customers to deploy small satellites weighing up to 975 lbs (443 kg) into low Earth orbit.

AGENA-B UPPER-STAGE LAUNCH VEHICLE. Used from 1959 until the mid-1980s as orbital injection vehicles or intermediate stage boosters for space probes.

HUMAN SPACEFLIGHT

SPACE SHUTTLE *ENTERPRISE*. From 1977 through 1979, NASA used this vehicle for approach and landing test flights in the atmosphere as well as vibration tests and launch pad fit checks on the ground.

GEMINI VII. Astronauts Frank Borman and James A. Lovell Jr. were launched into orbit aboard this spacecraft on December 4, 1965, the fourth such flight of the Gemini program. The mission showed that humans could live in weightlessness for two weeks.

Left: Pegasus was the first aircraft-launched rocket booster to carry satellites into space. Scores of missiles and rockets are displayed in the James S. McDonnell Space Hangar at the Udvar-Hazy Center. Below: The Space Shuttle *Enterprise* is the centerpiece of the James S. McDonnell Space Hangar.

ANDROID FOR SPACE TESTING. An articulated dummy used to support the development of spacesuits. It used both hydraulic and electrical actuators to replicate many of the joint motions of the human body with realistic forces.

SATURN V INSTRUMENT UNIT. Housed the guidance system for the Saturn V launch vehicle that carried astronauts to the Moon.

SPACE SCIENCE

"ANITA." A spider carried on Skylab for web formation experiments.

MARS PATHFINDER. Test model of the spacecraft that landed on the red planet on July 4, 1997, and undertook scientific investigation until September 1997.

Above: A human-sized, NASA-built android used for 1960s spacesuit testing is displayed in the Space Hangar at the Udvar-Hazy Center.

RITCHIE MIRROR GRINDING MACHINE. For grinding large mirrors that sat on a heavy, flat, rotating metal turntable.

VEGA PROBE. An engineering model of the Soviet spacecraft that flew by the planet Venus in June 1985 and launched scientific instruments into the Venusian atmosphere.

APPLICATION SATELLITES

CORONA BUCKET. A film return capsule recovered on May 25, 1972 from the last CORONA photoreconnaissance satellite mission. The "bucket" returned photos of the Soviet Union taken from space.

APPLICATIONS TECHNOLOGY SATELLITE-1. The first of a series of six satellites sponsored by NASA, for research in the new field of space communications.

COMPUTER, MASSIVELY PARALLEL PROCESSOR AND EXPANSION UNIT. With parallel processing, this computer offered much greater capability to manipulate data. It revolutionized the processing of vast amounts of remote sensing data from space.

SMALL ARTIFACTS

More than 500 smaller artifacts are exhibited in cases throughout the hangar, including advanced spacesuit prototypes; research crystals formed in orbit; sounding rocket payloads; space-themed toys from the 1950s and 1960s, and even borscht in tubes, prepared for Soviet cosmonauts.

Above: Among the hundreds of items displayed in glass cases are the helmet and gloves used in training by Apollo 15 astronaut James Irwin, and boots used by Mercury astronaut Gordon Cooper.

Left: "Anita," a spider used for web formation experiments aboard Skylab, is displayed in a blue bottle.

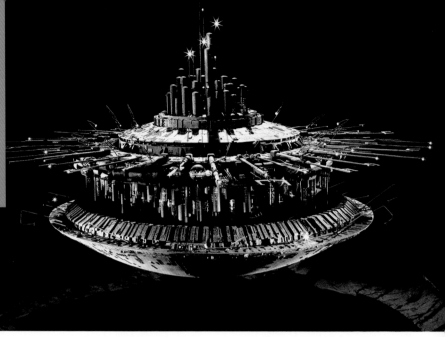

At the time of this guide's printing, the Udvar-Hazy Center was not completed. Depending on funding, the National Air and Space Museum plans to build a restoration hangar, archives, collections processing unit, conservation laboratory, and collections storage facility. Visitors will be able to view restorations in progress from the mezzanine level. These new facilities are scheduled to open in 2011.

Above: The mothership model used for the 1977 film *Close Encounters of the Third Kind* is among the more unusual artifacts found at the Udvar-Hazy Center.

GENERAL INFORMATION
(For the Mall building and Udvar-Hazy Center)

LOCATIONS
The National Mall building is at Independence Avenue and 6th Street, SW. Entrances: Independence Avenue and Jefferson Drive (on the Mall). The Steven F. Udvar-Hazy Center is near Washington-Dulles International Airport at 14390 Air and Space Museum Parkway, Chantilly, Virginia. The entrance is off Route 28.

HOURS
Open daily from 10:00 A.M. to 5:30 P.M. Closed on December 25.

GETTING THERE
• PUBLIC TRANSPORTATION: The closest Metrorail stop to the National Mall building is the L'Enfant Plaza station. Currently, there is no public transportation to the Udvar-Hazy Center from downtown. Virginia Regional Transit (VRTA) provides connecting bus service between Dulles International Airport,

Dulles Town Center and the Udvar-Hazy Center. Free transfers from other VRTA routes that transit the Dulles Town Center are available. Schedules, fares and information are available on the VRTA Web site at http://www.vatransit.org/bus_schedules.cfm. For more information call: 540-338-1610.

• BY CAR: The National Mall building does not have public parking, but there are many commercial parking lots in the area. Limited on-street parking is available, including handicapped spaces. At the Udvar-Hazy Center, parking is available for $15 a day. You can purchase an annual parking pass for $65 ($50 for National Air and Space Society members). Phone 703-572-4102 or e-mail uhcparkingpass@si.edu to purchase a pass.

VISITOR SERVICES

Welcome Centers are located near the entrances to both museums. For Smithsonian information call 202-633-1000 (voice) or 202-357-1729 (TTY). Send queries by e-mail to info@si.edu, or visit the Smithsonian Web site at www.si.edu.

TOURS

Highlight tours are given by Museum docents daily at 10:30 A.M. and 1:00 P.M. at both locations.

SCHOOLS: School group reservations for tours, programs, and science demonstrations must be made in writing at least three weeks in advance. Details are on the Web at www.nasm.si.edu. For reservations, use the online form at www/nasm.si.edu/tickets, call Monday through Friday 202-633-2563 (voice) or 202-357-1505 (TTY), fax 202-633-1957, or e-mail nasmtours@si.edu.

WHERE TO EAT

In the National Mall building: The Wright Place Food Court is on the first floor, just past Space Hall. At the Udvar-Hazy Center: A McDonald's and McCafé are on the entrance level.

SHOPPING

The museum stores are on the first floor near the entrance in the National Mall building, and on the entrance level at the Udvar-Hazy Center.

THEATERS

Large-format films are presented on giant screens in IMAX® theaters at both locations. Simulations of the night sky and programs on astronomy and space are presented in the Albert Einstein Planetarium in the National Mall building. For show information or to purchase tickets, visit www.nasm.si.edu or call 202-633-4629.

ACCESSIBILITY INFORMATION

Both locations offer access ramps and elevators. All theaters are wheelchair accessible, and most shows offer audio descriptions and/or closed captioning. Wheelchairs are available at both locations free of charge; inquire at the Welcome Center. Tours for persons who have visual, hearing, or other impairments may be arranged at least three weeks in advance by calling 202-633-2563.

WHAT'S UP

For monthly updates on Museum events, subscribe to the National Air and Space Museum's e-newsletter, What's Up, at www.nasm.si.edu.

The *Sant Ocean Hall* introduces visitors to the ocean as a dynamic global system essential to *all* life—past, present, and future.

NATIONAL MUSEUM OF NATURAL HISTORY

Accessible entrance:
Constitution Avenue
at 10th Street, N.W.
Mall entrance: Madison
Drive between 9th and
12th Streets, N.W.
Hours: Daily from
10 A.M. to 5:30 P.M.;
closed December 25.
Dining: Atrium Café,
Fossil Café,
Ice Cream Bar.
Metro: Smithsonian
and Federal
Triangle stations.
Smithsonian
information:
202-633-1000,
202-633-5285 (TTY) or
www.mnh.si.edu.

The National Museum of Natural History is dedicated to understanding the natural world and our place in it. As the nation's largest research museum, it is a treasure trove of more than 126 million natural and cultural objects. This encyclopedic collection serves as an essential resource for scientists studying earth sciences, the biological world, and human origins and cultures. Exhibitions and educational programs attract nearly 7 million visitors a year to the museum's green-domed Beaux Arts building, one of Washington's best known landmarks.

Only a tiny portion of the vast collections is on public display. Many of the objects are housed in the Smithsonian's Museum Support Center in Suitland, Maryland, a state-of-the-art facility for storage and conservation of research collections.

Seemingly endless drawers of insects surround Museum entomologists. There are more than 35 million insect specimens in the museum's collection.

Behind the scenes in the laboratories and offices at the museum and support center, more than 100 scientists conduct research in association with colleagues from universities, other museums, and government agencies.

The story told in the museum's exhibit halls is the story of our planet, from its fiery beginnings to its transformation over billions of years by a marvelous web of evolving life, including our own species. Living and nonliving, art and artifact—taken together, they reveal a wondrous and complex world.

GROUND FLOOR

A grand, two-story space, the Constitution Avenue Lobby features the museum's Easter Island ancestor figure, first put on exhibit in 1888, and jewel-like exhibit cases that highlight the museum's diverse collections. The 250 objects on display include amethyst and pyrite crystals, a 700,000-year-old hand ax from Kenya, pottery by renowned Pueblo artist Maria Martinez, Northwest Coast totem poles, a giant fossilized shark tooth, and a calcite-encrusted bird's nest.

The wide hallway beyond the lobby holds a huge stone disc from the Micronesian island of Yap in the South Pacific. The disc stands near the entrance to the Atrium Café and the glass elevator to the Samuel C. Johnson Theater where 2-D and 3-D IMAX® films are shown.

Baird Auditorium, used for lectures, concerts, films, and other special events, is also located on the ground floor. Just outside the auditorium, Baird Gallery displays nearly 300 mounted species of birds of the eastern United States, including some superb examples of hawks and eagles.

An Easter Island *moai* stands sentry at this Museum entrance.

The museum's African bull elephant welcomes visitors to the majestic four-story Rotunda. The diorama depicts his natural habitat in Angola.

FIRST FLOOR

ROTUNDA

Dominating the Rotunda, the Fénykövi elephant is the largest mounted elephant in the world. This African bull elephant—standing 13' 2" inches high at the shoulder and weighing close to 12 tons—towers over a slice of its native Angola. The plants and animals at its feet

are a combination of actual specimens, models, and casts that represent the museum's major scientific departments. A walk around the diorama reveals evidence of other life—animal tracks in the mud, dung beetles rolling away elephant waste, a jackal returning to its den, and the rib of a million-year-old elephant ancestor. Birds call, insects buzz, and the elephant trumpets on the hour from a surrounding soundscape.

On the second floor balcony encircling the Rotunda, interpretive exhibits look more closely at the elephant's anatomy, evolution, and role in African culture.

The eight-sided Rotunda is one of Washington, DC's most dramatic spaces, and many of its distinctive design elements are best seen from the balcony.

OCEAN

From the moment visitors arrive in the *Sant Ocean Hall,* they find themselves in another world. A gigantic whale dives overhead; panoramic underwater video footage wraps around the walls; a vast array of fossils, specimens, and habitats invites exploration. Earth, the exhibit shows, is an ocean planet, with much of its surface covered by a magnificent swath of blue. Though the ocean spans many basins, there is only one ocean, and it forms a global system essential to all life on earth—including yours!

Opened in 2008, the *Sant Ocean Hall* fills a magnificently restored gallery of the museum, becoming its

The *Sant Ocean Hall* ambassador, Phoenix, is modeled after an actual North Atlantic right whale living in the waters off the East Coast of the United States.

Visitors discover the ocean in all its complexity and unearthly beauty in the *Sant Ocean Hall*.

largest exhibition ever. Ongoing research and the museum's unparalleled collections anchor the exhibits; a mix of videos, interactive displays, and new technology for exploring the ocean draws visitors of all ages.

Phoenix, a model of an actual North Atlantic right whale tracked since birth, greets visitors. Descending through the soaring, two-story atrium, she is accurate in every detail. Only about 400 whales like her are left in the world. Below the giant model, a display of hunting and ceremonial artifacts from indigenous Arctic communities reflects their respect for the whale and her gifts of food, fuel, and bone. Three magnificent fossil whales nearby chart the whale's evolution and help carry visitors back to 3.5 billion years ago when the first life forms appeared in the sea. Over time, marine species rose and fell in bursts of adaptation and extinction as ocean ecosystems changed—a process captured by the dramatic murals and fossils in the "Journey through Time" gallery.

Two shows play at opposite ends of the hall— one in the Ocean Explorer Theater where visitors watch a manned submersible dive to the largely unknown sea floor, and the other on a 6-foot-wide globe suspended in the "Science on a Sphere" gallery. Data from satellite observations illuminate the surface of the sphere, showing how the ocean functions as one huge global system.

The hall also invites visitors to become ocean explorers. In the open ocean, they find marine organisms living in three layers: sunlit surface, twilight zone where food and light are scarce, and cold, dark ocean bottom. On the coastline—where humans impact the ocean most—a look beneath a beach blanket reveals an amazing variety of microscopic animals wedged between grains of sand. The 1,500-gallon aquarium holds a live Indo-Pacific reef with dozens of colorful species.

"Science on a Sphere," created by the National Oceanic and Atmospheric Administration, uses a dramatic multimedia presentation to explain many of the complex aspects of the ocean.

Ultimately, humans play a huge part in determining the fate of the ocean. Two computer programs— one on managing marine resources and the other about climate change—challenge viewers to think about the choices needed to safeguard this critical resource and usher in a new era of ocean stewardship.

HUMAN ORIGINS

Who are we? Who were our ancestors? When did they live?

The museum's groundbreaking *David H. Koch Hall of Human Origins*, open in 2010, explores these univer-

sal questions, showing how the characteristics that make us human evolved against a backdrop of dramatic climate change. The story begins 6 million years ago on the African continent where the earliest humans took the first steps toward walking upright. Since then, there have been over a dozen species of early humans, with multiple species often sharing the earth. All of them are now extinct—except for our own, *Homo sapiens.*

The hall tells this incredible story through more than 280 fossils, casts, and artifacts, many from the museum's own collections. Displayed alongside the research of the Smithsonian Human Origins program and other scientific institutions, these objects trace the evolutionary history of our small branch of the tree of life.

Visitors enter the hall through a time tunnel, seeing nine early human species appear and disappear and environments come and go. Along one large wall, a dramatic display of fossils, objects, videos, and images features some of the most significant "milestones" in becoming human: walking upright, making tools, evolving different body types and larger brains,

Above: This reconstruction of Shanidar 1, a male Neanderthal from Shanidar Cave, Iraq, was sculpted by John Gurche. Below: The exhibit displays many reproductions of Paleolithic paintings and sculptures, including the 17,000-year-old yellow "Chinese Horse," from Lascaux Cave, France.

developing social networks, and creating symbols and language.

Three displays recreate specific moments in the past and invite visitors to explore actual excavations. The braincase of a 1.8-million-year-old youth found in Swartkrans, South Africa, for example, still shows a leopard's fatal puncture marks. Visitors reconstruct the scene as they touch models of fossil "clues" from the site, and the life-and-death events of that fateful day long ago unfold in a time-lapse animation.

At the crossroads of the hall, a fascinating display of fossil skulls illustrates the history of human evolution. Nearby, eight lifelike faces stare out at visitors. It took artist John Gurche more than two years to sculpt the faces, using the latest forensic techniques, fossil discoveries, and his knowledge of human and ape anatomy.

Our species, *Homo sapiens*, evolved in East Africa by around 200,000 years ago, and then—as a world map of fossil discoveries shows—spread around the globe. Physical and cultural differences emerged as populations adapted to different habitats. Still, despite superficial variations in size, shape, skin, and eyes, the DNA of all modern humans differs by only 0.1 percent.

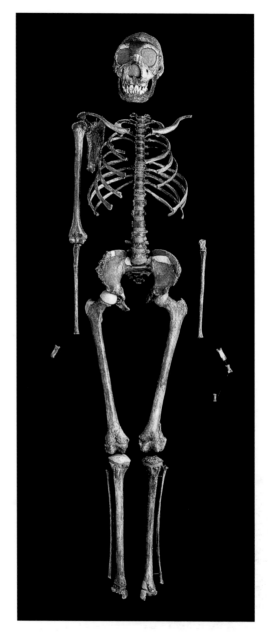

The skeleton of Turkana Boy, a juvenile *Homo erectus*, was found in 1.6-million-year-old sediments west of Lake Turkana, Kenya.

MAMMALS

The *Kenneth E. Behring Family Hall of Mammals* invites you to join the mammal family reunion in a dramatic hall restored to its impressive original architecture. Reopened in the fall of 2003 after a major renovation, the mammals hall presents the wondrous diversity of mammals and tells the story of how they adapted to a changing world. As this hall demonstrates, all mammals past and present —visitors included— are related to one another by virtue of common descent. Mammals belong to an ancient lineage that stretches back to before the time of dinosaurs. As living mammals, we all share certain characteristics that scientists use to identify this group. All mammals have hair, nurse on milk, and have a unique hearing apparatus that evolved from ancestral jawbones. We are all part of the great diversity of mammals. The hall combines a passionate and detailed commitment to scholarship with fresh interpretive approaches custom-designed to meet the needs of visitors. The exhibition features the museum's collections and takes full advantage of the exciting array of new interactive learning technologies, which allow for engaging and in-depth content. Designed with families in mind, the exhibit showcases taxidermy mammals in exciting, lifelike poses, features a wealth of hands-on

activities, and has an award-winning theater presentation on mammal evolution.

Visit the grassland, desert, and forest of Africa: get up close to a giraffe, see how lions hunt large prey, find out about bears that lived here more than five million years ago. Wander through Australia, where ancient mammals flourished; today it is the only place in the world inhabited by all three mammal groups: monotremes, marsupials, and placentals. Visit North America's far north and see how mammals protect themselves from the cold. Then travel to the North American prairie and discover how the pronghorn runs faster than any other living mammal and why bison are so well suited to this environment.

Discover the world of the Amazon rainforest, the earth's largest, where abundant plant life sets the stage for crowded living conditions. Find out how rain forest mammals make the most of these resources, from the shady forest floor to the canopy above.

If you really want to get to know your relatives, the *Kenneth E. Behring Hall of Mammals* is the place to go!

Above: A pouncing tiger is one of the 274 species of mammals that greet visitors to the *Kenneth E. Behring Family Hall of Mammals*. Opposite: North America's largest living carnivore, the brown bear looks similar to its 250,000-year-old ancestors.

Top: The *Triceratops* on display is the world's first totally digitized dinosaur. Bottom: Visitors witness the painstaking process of making casts from fragile fossils.

FOSSILS

From microscopic traces of early life to massive woolly mammoths, the museum's fossil halls trace the story of life on earth—a story that began nearly 3.5 billion years ago in the primordial seas that covered much of earth. Over the vast expanse of time, animals and plants gradually evolved into the millions of forms we see today. The more than 3,100 fossils in these halls preserve this incredible story.

One very special rock just inside the Early Life entrance to the hall—a cabbage-size specimen that resembles sediments produced by marine microorganisms today—may be the oldest-known direct evidence of life on earth. Close by, a large specimen from the famous Burgess Shale, discovered in 1910 by Charles D. Wolcott, fourth secretary of the Smithsonian, preserves fossils of soft-bodied animals in remarkable detail, giving a rare view into the past.

In the ancient seas, life came and went over millions of years. Two widespread extinctions doomed many kinds of marine life, and new species evolved to take their places—a dramatic story the exhibit explores in three acts with hundreds of fossils, a series of murals with the fossils fleshed out, and a detailed model of a 250-million-year-old reef. About 420 million years ago, plants began to colonize land, followed by animals. Look for the squat, fossilized stump of *Eospermatopteris,* one of the earliest known trees, in this area as well as skeletons of many amphibians—the first vertebrates to move onto land.

More than 30 of the museum's 1,500 dinosaur specimens reign over the soaring central gallery. An awesome predator and its potential prey, *Tyrannosaurus rex* and *Triceratops horridus,* face off at the gallery entrance. Beyond, a parade of colossal dinosaurs puts on a show. Not until dinosaurs died out did mammals take center stage. Rare early mammal specimens and mounted skeletons—many unearthed by Smithsonian scientists—stand against a backdrop of vivid murals. Nearby in FossiLab, museum staff and volunteers prepare fossils and give visitors a glimpse of what goes on behind the scenes in the museum.

Mounted skeletons of giant mammals dominate the Ice Age displays: a giant ground sloth, a woolly mammoth, an Irish elk. Rapid changes in climate and vegetation may have hastened their demise, but most likely hunting and other changes caused by the arrival of another mammal—*Homo sapiens*—drove them to extinction.

AFRICA

Rich and resonant voices from Africa and the African diaspora—together with objects both commonplace and extraordinary—express the complexity of African lives and cultures. Africa's most striking characteristics are its immense size and diverse cultures. More than three times larger than the continental United States, Africa today is home to more than a billion people inhabiting 54 countries. The African continent is divided by the boundaries of its nation-states as well as by diverse language groups, cultures, ecological zones, and histories.

The *African Voices* exhibit resonates with the dynamism of contemporary African culture. It examines the overlapping, continuously broadening spheres of

This 18th-century brass head of an *oba*, or king, comes from the Benin Kingdom, now a part of Nigeria. The opening on top once held a carved ivory tusk depicting the glories of the *oba*'s reign.

African influence—historical and contemporary, local and international—in the realms of family, work, commerce, and the natural environment. Objects such as a 17th-century cast brass head from the Benin Kingdom of Nigeria, a late-19th-century carved wooden staff by the Luba of Zaire, and decorative fiber headwear from 19th- and 20th-century Zaire show the aesthetic dimensions of leadership in certain African societies. A late-19th-century copper-and-brass image made by the Kota peoples of Gabon and a contemporary Afro-Brazillian altar demonstrate the enduring presence of African belief systems on the African continent and in Africa's diaspora. Akan gold weights, Ethiopian silver crosses, and decorated ceramic vessels show the history of metallurgy and pottery in different regions. Objects used in everyday life, contemporary fashion, children's toys, musical instruments, and excerpts from oral poetry, song, and literary texts illustrate the transatlantic connection between Africa and the Americas.

The platinum and diamond earrings of Marie Antoinette.

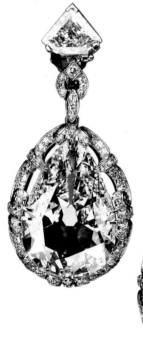

SECOND FLOOR
GEOLOGY, GEMS, AND MINERALS

The *Janet Annenberg Hooker Hall of Geology, Gems, and Minerals,* located off the second-floor Rotunda balcony, is the world's most comprehensive earth science complex. The legendary Hope diamond—a must-see for visitors—stars in the "Harry Winston Gallery." Surrounded by sparkling white diamonds, the 45.52-carat blue diamond rotates in a custom-made vault under precise fiber optic lighting. The gem is named for former owner Henry Philip Hope of England and is still in the setting made for Evelyn Walsh McLean of

Washington, DC, its last private owner. The New York jewelry firm, Harry Winston, Inc., acquired the famous diamond in 1949 and donated it to the Smithsonian in 1958.

The "Harry Winston Gallery" also features five other wonders of nature: enormous quartz crystals from Africa, one of the largest sheets of naturally occurring copper in existence, a sandstone formation sculpted by water within the earth, polished gneiss born from heat and pressure deep below the surface, and a ring-shaped meteorite from another world.

The "National Gem Collection" includes the Marie Antoinette earrings, the 127-carat Portuguese diamond, the Carmen Lúcia ruby, and the Hooker starburst diamonds.

The 2,500 specimens in the "Gems and Minerals Gallery" include spectacular crystal pockets, a dazzling selection of gems, and crystals that have grown in amazing and unusual ways. In the "Rocks Gallery," each specimen represents a bit of earth's history and shows how rocks bend, break, melt, and transform into other kinds of rocks over time. Intense heat from within the earth drives the movement of rocky plates at the surface—the process highlighted in the "Plate Tectonics Gallery" with a giant globe, specimens from volcanoes and earthquakes, a volcano study station, and a theater. Completing the hall, the "Moon, Meteorites, and Solar System Gallery" features Moon rocks, a touchable Mars meteorite, an extensive display of other meteorites, and tiny bits of stardust from the cloud that gave birth to the Sun.

Above: The 45.52-carat Hope diamond is the best-known and largest blue diamond in the world. Below: This case houses a rare Moon rock. This display is one of a series that shows the different stages in the Moon's evolution.

BUTTERFLIES + PLANTS

No matter what season you visit, it feels like a picture-perfect summer day inside the Butterfly Pavilion. Hundreds of butterflies and moths flutter from flower to flower, sip nectar, roost, and flex their wings. Small chrysalides hang in the Transformation Station just as they would in nature while caterpillars' tissues reorganize and adult butterflies take shape. The butterflies and moths come in a stunning variety of colors and patterns, which helps protect them from predators. Look for moths that match the bark where they roost, conspicuous wing patterns that advertise a bitter taste, and eye spots on wings that help frighten away birds and lizards. Tickets for the pavilion are available at www.butterflies.si.edu, by phone at 202-633-4629, or at the pavilion box office.

There is no charge to see the many other butterfly displays in *Partners in Evolution: Butterflies + Plants,* where visitors discover more about how butterflies and moths live and how they evolved with plants over hundreds of millions of years. Sometimes butterflies and plants interact as friends—sometimes as foes. Take the yucca moth and yucca plant. For some 40

A rose swallowtail butterfly in profile.

This Ulysses swallowtail butterfly is native to Australia.

million years, yucca moths have played an active role in fertilizing yucca plants while depositing their eggs in the yucca flower's ovaries. Milkweed plants, however, defend themselves against insect invaders with milky sap that sticks to mouthparts and bodies. Milkweed beetles have evolved a behavior that avoids the sap by cutting into leaf veins and letting the latex drain out so they can feed.

A series of murals and rare plant and insect fossils paint images of earth in four different time periods, showing how tens of millions of years of evolution produced the amazing diversity of butterflies and moths seen today. Along the way, many species died out, while others endured, eventually giving rise to the specialized day-flying moths we now call butterflies.

A display near the Rotunda entrance gives a sense of just how large the museum's plant, insect, and fossil collections are, and the critical role they play as museum scientists work to unravel the mysteries of evolution.

Above: At the popular O. Orkin Insect Zoo, you can get close enough to see the hairs on a tarantula. Tarantulas use these hairs to locate prey. Below: The massive skeleton of a Steller sea cow—perhaps the most complete such skeleton in existence—looms over skeletons of meat-eating animals. It was assembled from bones salvaged on Bering Island in 1883.

INSECT ZOO

The whirls, chirps, buzzes, and rattles heard at the entrance to the *O. Orkin Insect Zoo* are the sounds of earth's most abundant, diverse, and successful animals—insects and their relatives. They have adapted extraordinarily well to environments all over the world. The popular walk-through tropical rainforest displays live giant cockroaches found in forest litter and tree hollows. In another part of the display, look for cave arthropods and other invertebrates attracted by constant year-round temperature and moisture.

The interactive exhibits and participatory activities in the Insect Zoo invite visitors of all ages to explore and get involved. Children can crawl through a large model of an African termite mound, examine a real beehive, or hold a hissing cockroach. Tarantula feedings take place several times a day.

REPTILES AND AMPHIBIANS

A life-size habitat re-creates the Florida Everglades—home to alligators, tree frogs, turtles, and a variety of snakes, including the diamondback rattlesnake. The Giants case features the world's largest lizard, the Komodo dragon, which can reach nearly 10 feet. Just above is the reticulated python, the largest of all pythons, which commonly grows to 23 feet. Other cases look at defensive strategies, reptile and amphibian growth and development, and the impact of human economics on reptiles and amphibians.

BONES

Hundreds of skeletons of mammals, birds, reptiles, amphibians, and fishes—ranging from a gigantic, extinct Steller sea cow to a tiny pocket mouse—are exhibited in characteristic poses and grouped by order to illustrate their relationships. Exhibits also show how bone structures evolved in adaptation to environment. Zebras, for example, have elongated lower leg and foot bones that enable them to outrun predators on open African savannas. The massive leg bones of the hippopotamus are built to support its huge body.

Komodo dragons live on several Indonesian islands where they climb trees, swim, and chase down prey.

KOREA

Thousands of years ago, on a peninsula in East Asia, the distinctive culture and language of Korea arose. The *Korea Gallery* features several traditions that help define the country's strong national identity, using artifacts from the museum and other collections from around the world.

Elegantly presented in front of Korean latticework, a chronological display of ceramics, including classic Korean celadons, helps put Korea's long history in context. Contemporary wedding garments illustrate distinctive wedding traditions. Other displays explore Korean ancestor worship and Hangeul, the unique syllabic writing system of Korea.

Just outside the gallery, contemporary Korean art shows how the rich traditions of the past still provide inspiration for a dynamic, modern Korea.

SPECIAL EXHIBITS

There's always something new to see at the museum. From world-class photography displays to fascinating archeological finds that illuminate understanding of the past, the National Museum of Natural History offers an exciting roster of changing exhibitions every year. These exhibits amplify the museum's mission of understanding the natural world and our place in it, and complement its research and educational goals.

The museum hosts traveling exhibits from other institutions as well as those developed by our own exhibits and curatorial staff. Many of these exhibits

reflect the cutting-edge science and research conducted here at the museum.

Come back often to see what new exhibits the museum has in store for you.

WESTERN CULTURES

In *Origins of Western Cultures*, lifelike dioramas and nearly 2,500 objects help trace the development of Western civilization from about 10,000 years ago to A.D. 500.

After the Ice Age, nomadic people in southwestern Asia began to see the advantages of herding over hunting and growing over gathering plants. A diorama recreates one of the earliest known farming communities—Ali Kosh in Iran. The spread of agriculture also brought technological advances, represented by a diversity of tools, weapons, and pottery from sites in Europe.

Then, as cities began to emerge and urban life evolved, new forms of political and social organization led to the creation of states and, eventually, empires. Burial customs reflect the complexity of some of these ancient societies. In the Egypt display, a male mummy nicknamed "Minister Cox" appears in his original wrappings and coffin. A video about Smithsonian investigations of Bronze Age tombs at Bab-edh-Dhra in Jordon plays in the Gilgamesh Theater. Pottery and stone tools from Troy, Luristan bronzes, a Cycladic figurine, Etruscan bronzes, Greek pottery, and Roman glass, mosaic, and money represent many ancient empires.

The Iceman exhibit re-creates one of the most important archaeological finds of the 20th century—a 5,300-year-old ice "mummy" found remarkably intact in the Alps in 1991. The display includes a photomural about the discovery, reproductions of his clothing and tools, and a reconstruction of his body and head—all based on the actual remains and artifacts.

Above: The Iceman reconstruction shows how he might have looked in life. Opposite above: Carved wooden *sotdae* are traditionally erected at Korean village entrances to protect the community against calamities. Opposite below: Smithsonian forensic anthropologist Doug Owsley examines a burial in Jamestown, Virginia. The Smithsonian's work in Jamestown is featured in the special exhibit, *Written in Bone: Forensic Files of the 17th-Century Chesapeake.*

Examination of the body revealed cuts in his hand and an arrowhead in his back, two clues that confirm the Iceman spent his last moments in a fight for his life.

FORCES OF CHANGE

Nearly every scientific and social issue confronting us today relates to change. Understanding and adapting to these changes—whether they involve climate change ecological change, or cultural change—present critical challenges.

The museum's Forces of Change program explores these complex issues, looking at the intimate and often surprising connections between seemingly unrelated natural forces through outreach activities, a Web portal (http://forces.si.edu/), a book, and exhibits. The exhibits focus on diverse topics such as El Niño, earth's atmosphere, the Arctic, and prairie ecosystems.

In every exhibit, cultural and natural objects from the museum's collections provide tangible evidence of change. Interpretive stations and computer interactives highlight current scientific research and show how the forces of nature affect our lives.

"El Niño's Powerful Reach" was the Forces of Change premiere exhibit.

JOHNSON IMAX® THEATER

The lights go down, the show begins, and you are in another part of the world, far from Washington, DC. Perhaps you dive to the ocean depths for close encounters with some of the world's most exotic marine mammals; you might travel back to the age of the dinosaurs, coming face-to-face with some of earth's largest creatures ever. Whatever the topic, the theater's six-story screen, 3-D technology, and state-of-the-art sound system provide a truly memorable experience for the entire family.

The IMAX® films offered at the museum tell stories that revolve around our collections and exhibits, from oceans to dinosaurs to human evolution. The Samuel C. Johnson IMAX® Theater operates daily during regular museum hours. Schedules, feature information, and tickets are available at 202-633-4629 and www.si.edu/imax.

GENERAL INFORMATION

INFORMATION SERVICES

The visitor information desks, located at the Constitution Avenue entrance and in the Rotunda, are staffed by volunteers daily from 10 A.M. to 4 P.M. Also look for an information kiosk near the museum stores on the ground floor. Call 202-633-1000 (voice) or 202-633-5285 (TTY), or go online to www.mnh.si.edu.

ACCESSIBILITY

The wheelchair accessible entrance is at 10th and Constitution Avenue. Accessibility information for the Smithsonian Institution is available at www.si.edu/visit/visitors_with_ disabilities.htm, by telephone at 202-633-2921 (voice) or 202-633-4353 (TTY). Baird Auditorium offers loop amplification in the center front rows, and assistive listening devices are available at the IMAX® Theater. For special services for groups, call 202-633-1077 (voice) or fax 202-786-2778.

DINING

The 600-seat Atrium Café in the Discovery Center on the ground floor offers hamburgers, hot dogs, French fries, pizza, roast chicken, pasta, submarine sandwiches, salads, ice cream, desserts, beverages, and other lunch items in a casual atmosphere. The Fossil Café in the dinosaur hall on the first floor offers espressos, lattes, cookies, muffins, salads, and light snacks.

MUSEUM STORES

The main museum store on the ground floor carries a variety of Smithsonian souvenirs and gifts related to natural history. Across the hall is a store especially appealing to children. Theme-oriented shops elsewhere in the museum feature books and memorabilia relating to exhibitions.

DISCOVERY ROOM

On the first floor is a family-oriented education facility featuring multi-sensory experiences with objects from the world of nature. Please consult the museum website at www.mnh.si.edu for Discovery Room hours, programming, and other recommendations. All children visiting the Discovery Room must be accompanied by an adult.

SAMUEL C. JOHNSON IMAX® THEATER

Check the museum's website or call 202-633-IMAX (4629) for schedules and ticketing information. For groups, call 866-868-7774. For online information and sales, go to www.si.edu/imax.

LIVE BUTTERFLY PAVILION

Open daily 10:15 A.M., to 5 P.M., Tickets required; available online at www.butterflies.si.edu/tickets, by phone at 202-633-4629 (voice) or 877-932-4629 (TTY), and at the pavilion box office. Tuesdays free, but timed-entry ticket required.

LIVE DEMONSTRATIONS

Tarantula feedings, *O. Orkin Insect Zoo,* Tuesdays through Fridays, 10:30 A.M., 11:30 A.M., and 1:30 P.M.; Saturdays and Sundays, 11:30 A.M., 12:30 P.M., and 1:30 P.M.

From the Constituion Avenue Lobby, a hall leads past a *rai,* a symbol of status on the Micronesian Island of Yap.

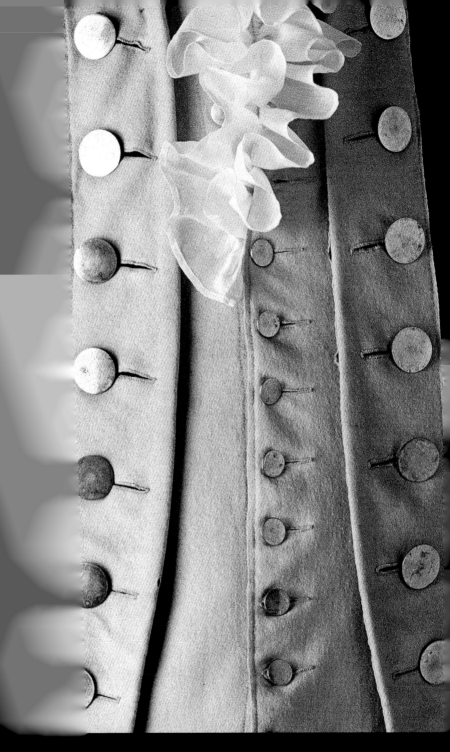

al George Washington began wearing this uniform coat around

e had resigned from the Continental Army to become the nation's

-chief. Opposite top: The "Teddy bear" was created by the Ideal Toy

NATIONAL MUSEUM OF AMERICAN HISTORY, KENNETH E. BEHRING CENTER

In 1858, the "objects of art and of foreign and curious research" in the National Cabinet of Curiosities were transferred from the U.S. Patent Office to the Smithsonian Institution. This was the genesis of the collections in the National Museum of American History. After the Centennial Exposition of 1876 closed, the Smithsonian received a windfall of objects that had been displayed in Philadelphia for the nation's 100th anniversary celebration. Many of those objects were put on exhibit in the US National Museum Building (now the Arts and Industries Building) when it opened in 1881. Today, the spacious halls of the National Museum of American History are filled with exhibits that explore America's social, cultural, scientific, and technological history.

IF SO CAN YOU SE
WHAT SO PROUDLY
WHOSE BROAD STR
O'ER THE RAMPART
AND THE ROCKET'S
GAVE PROOF THRO
O! SAY, DOES THAT
O'ER THE LAND OF

The flag that inspired the national anthem is displayed at the heart of the museum in a specially constructed gallery.

SHINING NEW LIGHT ON AMERICAN HISTORY

The National Museum of American History recently completed a dramatic transformation of the building's center core. Visitors connect to the American story as they walk into the central atrium with a new skylight that dramatically opens the building and a grand staircase that connects the museum's first and second floors. Extensive 10-foot-high "artifact walls" on both the first and second floors showcase changing displays from the breadth of the museum's three million objects which represent the nation's heritage in the areas of science, technology, sociology and popular culture. A Welcome Center on the second floor and Information Desk on the first floor provide visitors with orientation in the museum. Six Landmark Objects permanently serve as thematic heralds and way-finding features to the exhibition wings.

Please visit the museum's Web site at americanhistory.si.edu for up-to-date information about exhibitions and public programs. At this site, visitors can also subscribe to a free monthly electronic newsletter. For Smithsonian information, please call 202-633-1000.

FIRST FLOOR

EAST WING: TRANSPORTATION AND TECHNOLOGY
WEST WING: SCIENCE AND INNOVATION

AMERICA ON THE MOVE

This 26,000-square-foot exhibition anchors the General Motors Hall of Transportation and features more than 300 transportation artifacts—from the 1903 Winton that was the first car to be driven across the U.S. to the 199-ton, 92-foot-long "1401" locomotive, to a 1970s shipping container—all showcased in period settings.

SMITHSONIAN INSTITUTION LIBRARIES GALLERY

The Smithsonian Institution Libraries Exhibition Gallery is located on the first floor, in the west wing, of the National Museum of American History. Guest curated by Smithsonian staff, the exhibitions showcase books from the Libraries' rich and diverse collections. For more information, see page 20."

The Fredonia's deep hull, narrow beam, and fine lines represent the pinnacle of design for deepwater fishing schooners. In 1896, the *Fredonia* was hit by a heavy sea and sank.

The exhibition's 19 settings, organized chronologically, allow visitors the opportunity to travel back in time and experience transportation as it shaped American lives and landscapes. As visitors travel through the show, they can walk on 40 feet of Route 66's original pavement from Oklahoma or board a 1950s Chicago Transit Authority Car and, through multi-media technology, experience a "commute" into downtown Chicago on a December morning.

ON THE WATER

Maritime trade established major cities, created connections between people and places, and opened the continent. A new permanent 8,000-square-foot exhibition about the country's maritime history and culture, "On the Water: Stories from Maritime

America" engages the public in a dynamic exploration of America's maritime past and present through objects, video and interactive stations.

JOHN BULL LOCOMOTIVE
LANDMARK OBJECT – TRANSPORTATION
AND TECHNOLOGY

The oldest operable, self-propelled locomotive in the world, the *John Bull* became a symbol of the Industrial Revolution. Built in England and brought to America in 1831 for service on the Camden and Amboy Railroad of New Jersey, one of the first public railroads in the U.S., the *John Bull* was an English design modified to fit the expansion of a frontier nation. The locomotive transported passengers from two of America's largest cities, Philadelphia and New York.

LIGHTING A REVOLUTION

Thomas Edison's revolutionary invention is only the beginning of the story of electricity, which is the subject of this exhibition. Here, visitors can explore the similarities and differences between the process of invention in Edison's era and today.

POWER MACHINERY

The full-size engines and models displayed here illustrate the harnessing of atmospheric forces, the early age of steam power, and the development of high-pressure and high-speed engines. Displays show the evolution of steam boilers and the steam turbine, and progress in the techniques of harnessing waterpower. The collection also includes a number of historic internal-combustion engines.

STORIES ON MONEY

"Stories on Money" explores the museum's National Numismatic Collection through two different themes. "America's Money" examines how money changed from colonial days to the present, featuring objects from Colonial America and the Gold Rush,

Above: A Thomas Edison lightbulb, early 1880. Opposite Below: The John Bull was a symbol of the Industrial Revolution and an engine of change. Built in England and brought to America in 1831, the John Bull is the world's oldest, operable, self-propelled locomotive. The Bull transported passengers from Philadelphia and New York City and set the style for American locomotives to come. Left: This ten dollar coin was made in 1850 by Baldwin & Company during the gold rush. The cowboy design celebrates the spirit of the western frontier.

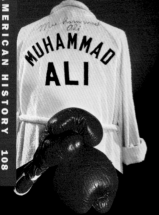

AT A GLANCE

The Star-Spangled Banner, the First Ladies' gowns, Abraham Lincoln's hat, Lewis and Clark's compass, Muhammad Ali's boxing gloves, Thomas Jefferson's wooden portable desk on which he wrote the Declaration of Independence, the *John Bull* locomotive, Kermit the Frog—the list of America's favorites could go on and on in this wide-ranging, entertaining, and educational museum.

and explores the renaissance of American coinage. "The Power of Liberty" features an array of liberty coins from the United States and around the world as well as coins featuring real and mythological women. The exhibition immerses the visitors in objects and interactive media where visitors can view enlarged images and delve further into numismatic history.

BON APPÉTIT! JULIA CHILD'S KITCHEN AT THE SMITHSONIAN

Visitors at the National Museum of American History can sneak a peek into chef Julia Child's legendary Cambridge, Massachusetts, kitchen. When Child moved back to her home state of California in 2001, she donated the contents of her 14-foot by 20-foot custom-designed kitchen, including small utensils, personal cookbooks, the stainless steel kitchen sink, and her six-burner Garland commercial range. The kitchen, which Child used as the set of three television shows and as the testing ground for many recipes featured in her cookbooks, is composed of more than 1,200 individual pieces. The museum staff packed and catalogued everything, then reassembled it in the museum exactly as it was in Child's home.

"INVENTION AT PLAY" IN THE JEROME AND DOROTHY LEMELSON HALL OF INVENTION GALLERY

How was the Post-it Note invented? Why do we use Velcro? Who thought up the idea for microwave ovens? Visitors of all ages can learn about the inventors and trace the paths to their discoveries while enjoying puzzles, experiments, and hands-on activities.

SCIENCE IN AMERICAN LIFE

In modern America, science and society are inseparable. Over the last 125 years, scientific research and science-based technology have been the most powerful agents of change in American life, and science has grown into a complex enterprise interwoven with all aspects of our culture. Through artifacts, historical photographs, and multimedia technology, this exhibition focuses on many of the scientific issues, achievements, misunderstandings, and controversies that have shaped contemporary life.

A recent addition to the exhibition's "Looking Ahead" gallery is "Robots on the Road," a display that explores how American society will react to recent research and innovations on mobile robots. The gallery features "Stanley," a modified blue 2005 Volkswagen Touareg, the winner of the 2005 Grand Challenge, a robot race sponsored by the Defense Advanced Research Projects Agency.

SPARK!LAB

Everybody can envision the "Eureka!" moment of invention, when the idea suddenly strikes and—BOOM—there's a new product ready to change the world. "Spark!Lab" is a hands-on space for visitors of all ages that features games, science experiments, inventors' notebooks and includes a special section for kids under five.

VASSAR TELESCOPE
LANDMARK OBJECT – SCIENCE AND INNOVATION WING

This telescope was used by Maria Mitchell, America's first woman astronomer and the first woman scientist of note at Vassar College. The lens has a diameter of 12 3/8 inches, making it the third largest refracting telescope in America at the time it was created. In addition, the telescope's equatorial mount, meaning that it has one rotational axis parallel to the Earth's axis of rotation, allowed it to be aligned with Earth's poles. This enabled the telescope to follow the motion of stars and planets across the sky.

Left: The telescope was used by Maria Mitchell, America's first woman astronomer and first woman scientist of note.

SECOND FLOOR

EAST WING: AMERICAN IDEALS
WEST WING: AMERICAN LIVES

STAR-SPANGLED BANNER GALLERY

The museum is home to the Star-Spangled Banner, the flag that inspired the national anthem. Visitors are able to view the flag in an atmosphere reminiscent of the "dawn's early light," similar to what Francis Scott Key experienced on the morning of Sept. 14, 1814, and learn about its history and preservation.

WELCOME CENTER

The Nina and Ivan Selin Welcome Center, adjacent to the Mall entrance, helps visitors make the most of their time at the museum by providing easy access to information about exhibitions, tours, and programs, as well as amenities.

A family visits the new Star-Spangled Banner Gallery and experiences the flag that inspired the national anthem in an atmosphere evoking "Dawns Early Light."

GEORGE WASHINGTON STATUE
LANDMARK OBJECT – AMERICAN LIVES

This marble statue of George Washington was sculpted by Horatio Greenough under commission by the United States government in 1832. Designed as an allusion to Phidias' "Olympian Zeus," the sculpture was originally unveiled in the Capitol rotunda in 1841 and was later moved to the Capitol lawn. The statue came to the Smithsonian in 1908 and debuted in this building in 1964.

FIRST LADIES AT THE SMITHSONIAN

A showcase of premier objects from the century-old collection, including 14 dresses ranging from Martha Washington to Laura Bush. The centerpiece of the gallery is a large exhibit case that features selected gowns, portraits, White House china, personal possessions, and associative objects from the Smithsonian's unique collection of first ladies material. A section discussing the tradition of the first lady's inaugural gown coming to the Smithsonian will answer some of the public's most frequently asked questions. It highlights the gown worn by Helen Taft (the first inaugural gown presented by the first lady herself in 1912) and the 2001 inaugural gown worn by Laura Bush.

COMMUNITIES IN A CHANGING NATION: THE PROMISE OF 19TH-CENTURY AMERICA

"Communities in a Changing Nation" examines the promise of America in the 1800s through the experiences of three different communities. Visitors will walk through the industrial era in Bridgeport, Connecticut; relive the Jewish immigrant experience in Cincinnati, Ohio; and witness slavery and freedom among African Americans in Charleston, South Carolina.

WITHIN THESE WALLS . . .

"Within These Walls . . ." tells the history of a house that stood at 16 Elm Street in Ipswich, Massachusetts, and five of the many families who occupied it from the mid-1760s through 1945. The exhibition explores some of the important ways ordinary people, in their daily lives, have been part of the great changes and events in American history. The centerpiece is the largest artifact in the museum, a Georgian-style, 2 1/2–story timber-framed house built in the 1760s, saved from the bulldozer by the citizens of Ipswich in 1963, and relocated to this space

Above: The first known photo of the Star-Spangled Banner, taken at the Boston Navy Yard in 1873. Below: A 2 ½ –story timber-framed house from 1760 was brought to the museum from Ipswich, Massachusetts, in 1963 and is the centerpiece of the exhibition "Within These Walls . . ."

On February 1, 1960, four African American students refused to leave the F.W. Woolworth's store lunch counter in Greensboro, North Carolina when they were denied service. Their defiance heightened many Americans' awareness of racial injustice and ultimately led to the desegregation of the counter.

within the museum. Within this house from Ipswich, American colonists created new ways of living, patriots sparked a Revolution, an African American struggled for freedom, community activists organized to end slavery, immigrants built new identities for themselves, and a grandmother and her grandson served on the home front during World War II.

GREENSBORO LUNCH COUNTER
LANDMARK OBJECT – AMERICAN IDEALS

On February 1, 1960, four African American students sat down at this counter and asked for service. They remained in their seats even though they were refused service and asked to leave. Their "passive sit-down demand" began the first sustained sit-in and ignited a youth-led movement to challenge injustice and inequality throughout the South. This defiant movement heightened many Americans' awareness of racial injustice and ultimately led to the desegregation of the F.W. Woolworth lunch counter on July 25, 1960.

NMAAHC GALLERY, CHANGING DISPLAYS

Until the Smithsonian's National Museum of African American History and Culture building has been completed in 2015, the new museum has a home in this gallery and will present changing exhibitions illustrating the major periods of African American history. Check the Web site for current information.

ALBERT H. SMALL DOCUMENTS GALLERY

This new intimate gallery allows the museum to show changing displays of fragile documents and photographs. Check the Web site for current information.

THIRD FLOOR

EAST WING: AMERICAN WARS AND POLITICS
WEST WING: ENTERTAINMENT, SPORTS, AND MUSIC

THE AMERICAN PRESIDENCY: A GLORIOUS BURDEN

"The American Presidency: A Glorious Burden" looks at the personal, public, ceremonial, and executive actions of the men who have held this office and impacted the course of history in the past 200 years. More than 900 artifacts, including national treasures from the Smithsonian's vast presidential collections, bring to life the role of the presidency in American culture. Among the exhibition's highlights are Thomas Jefferson's wooden lap desk on which he wrote the Declaration of Independence; the carriage Ulysses S. Grant rode to his second inauguration; the top hat worn by Abraham Lincoln the night of his assassination; George Washington's battle sword; Bill Clinton's military case used to contain the topmost national security information.

Above: Franklin D. Roosevelt used this microphone for his "fireside chats." Below: Thomas Jefferson drafted the Declaration of Independence on this portable desk. 1865.

ABRAHAM LINCOLN: AN EXTRAORDINARY LIFE (THROUGH JANUARY 2011)

This exhibition brings together the museum's unique Lincoln collection of more than 60 historical treasures for the first time. Through nationally important Lincoln artifacts and personal stories, visitors explore the life and times of this extraordinary figure.

THE PRICE OF FREEDOM: AMERICANS AT WAR

This 18,000-square-foot exhibition surveys the history of the U.S. military from the Colonial era to the present, exploring ways that wars have been defining episodes in American History. Using a unique blend of more than 800 original artifacts, graphic images, and interactive stations, the exhibition tells the story of how Americans have fought to establish the nation's independence, determine its borders, shape its values of freedom and opportunity, and define its leading role in world affairs.

Among the objects included in the exhibition are one of the few Revolutionary War uniforms in existence; furniture used by Gen. Ulysses S. Grant and Robert E. Lee during the surrender ceremony at Appomattox Court House; a restored Huey Helicopter, an icon of the Vietnam War and the largest object on display; and the uniform worn by Colin Powell during Operation Desert Storm.

Above: Uniform worn by Brigadier General Peter Gansevoort during the American Revolution. This is one of the few Revolutionary War uniforms in existence. Opposite: Abraham Lincoln wore this suit comprising a black broadcloth coat, trousers and vest during his presidency. The hat is the one he wore to Ford's Theatre the night of his assassination. Below: One of the famous Vietnam-era UH-1H "Huey" helicopters.

The Continental fleet's gunboat *Philadelphia*, which sank in battle in 1776, was discovered and raised from Lake Champlain in 1935.

GUNBOAT *PHILADELPHIA*

In October 1776, American troops in a ragtag collection of newly built boats faced an advancing line of British ships on Lake Champlain in New York. The Americans, under the command of Benedict Arnold, were forced to retreat, but not before they fought the British to a standstill. One of the American vessels, *Philadelphia*, sank during the battle and rested on the bottom of the lake until 1935. It was recovered that year with much of its equipment intact, and came to the Museum in 1964, complete with the 24-pound ball that sent the gunboat to the bottom.

CLARA BARTON/RED CROSS AMBULANCE

LANDMARK OBJECT – AMERICAN WARS AND POLITICS

This ambulance is one of eleven vehicles purchased in 1898 by the Central Cuban Relief Committee of New York for use by Clara Barton and the American National Red Cross. Commissioned and sent to Camp Thomas in Georgia right before the outbreak of the Spanish-American War, the ambulance was used to care for US Army soldiers before their deployment to Cuba. Later, Barton used the ambulance at her Maryland home, which served as the Red Cross headquarters, storehouse, and distribution center.

The ambulance is one of eleven vehicles purchased by the Central Cuban Relief Committee of New York for use by Clara Barton, before the outbreak of the Spanish-American War that year.

**Jim Henson's Kermit the
Frog, 1970.**

POPULAR CULTURE SELECTIONS: MUSIC,
SPORTS, AND ENTERTAINMENT HISTORY
Music, sports, and entertainment play major roles in
American life, shaping our national memory and often
defining what is American to the nation and to the
world. The memorable objects and ideas in this display
are a sampling of more than a century of collecting at
the Smithsonian. It features Dorothy's ruby slippers
from "The Wizard of Oz," Muhammad Ali and Joe
Louis' boxing gloves, and a boom box owned by hip
hop pioneer Fab 5 Freddy. (Objects on display are subject to change.)

DOLL HOUSE

Faith Bradford donated this dollhouse to the Smithsonian in 1951 after spending more than a half century collecting and building its miniature furnishings. The house is inhabited by Peter Doll, his wife Rose Washington Doll, and their ten children.

DUMBO
LANDMARK OBJECT – ENTERTAINMENT, MUSIC, SPORTS

Walt Disney's innovative theme park allowed this father of American entertainment to translate his iconic characters and stories into three dimensional, real-life experiences that transport park visitors into their beloved movie settings. Inspired by a 1939 children's book, the film version of "Dumbo" premiered in movie theaters in October 1941. The Disneyland attraction inspired by the film opened in August 1955 and endures as one of the park's most popular attractions.

In 2005, this aviating elephant from the Disneyland attraction "Dumbo the Flying Elephant" was presented to the Museum on the occasion of the 50th anniversary of Disneyland.

Antonio Stradivari (1644?-1737) of Cremona, Italy crafted a number of decorated string instruments. The instruments are well known as the *Ole Bull*, a violin made in 1687, the *Greffuhle* violin from 1709, the *Axelrod* viola built in 1695, and the *Marylebone* cello of 1688.

MUSICAL INSTRUMENTS

The *Hall of Musical Instruments* presents samples of instruments and music relating to the history, performance styles and techniques of European and American music and the development of musical instruments. Included in the hall are several instruments made by Antonio Stradivari, universally acknowledged to have been the greatest of all violin makers. While generally on display, these instruments also are used for performances of the Smithsonian Chamber Music Society.

LOWER LEVEL

TAKING AMERICA TO LUNCH

"Taking America to Lunch" celebrates the history of American lunch boxes. After reaching the height of their popularity at the dawn of the television era, lunch box sales became barometers for what was hip in popular culture at any point in time. Included in the display are approximately 75 objects drawn from the museum's collection of children's and workers' illustrated metal lunch boxes and beverage containers dating from the 1880s through the 1980s.

GENERAL INFORMATION

For information and maps, visit the Welcome Center on the second floor or the Information Desk on the first floor.

PUBLIC PROGRAMS, TOURS AND DEMONSTRATIONS

The museum offers tours and public programs daily. For information about tours, concerts, lectures, demonstrations and other activities, inquire at the Welcome Center or Information Desk, call 202-633-1000 or 202-357-1729 (TTY), or visit the museum's Web site at americanhistory.si.edu.

For inquiries about school tours, call 202-633-3717 or visit the Web site http://americanhistory.si.edu.

WHERE TO EAT

The Stars and Stripes Café offers a variety of all-American favorites on the Lower Level. In Constitution Café on the first floor, visitors can enjoy light fare, espresso, and hand-dipped ice-cream with a view onto bustling Constitution Avenue.

MUSEUM STORES

Museum stores are located on the first and second floors, offering a wide variety of objects and publications relating to American History plus postcards, film, T-shirts, and posters.

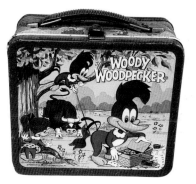

For generations, the lunch containers many of us hauled to school and work have reflected American culture. Of all the bags, boxes, trays, cans, and cartons we have carried over the past century, the most message-laden is the metal lunch box. A selection of boxes and their drink containers from the collections of the National Museum of American History explores this colorful heritage.

Mixtec-Aztec
Shield, 15th c.

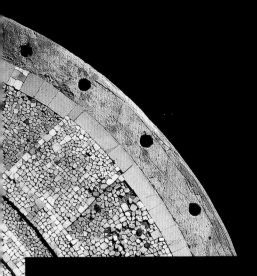

NATIONAL MUSEUM OF
THE AMERICAN INDIAN

The National Museum of the American Indian is an institution of living cultures dedicated to advancing knowledge and understanding of the life, languages, literature, history, and arts of the Native peoples of the Americas.

The museum is housed in three facilities: the National Museum of the American Indian on the National Mall in Washington, DC; the George Gustav Heye Center in New York City; and the Cultural Resources Center in Suitland, Maryland (open by appointment only).

Opposite: Shuar *Akitiai* (ear ornaments), Upper Amazon, Ecuador. Collected in 1935. Below, clockwise from lower left: Storyteller bracelet, by Joseph Coriz, Santo Domingo Pueblo, ca. 1990; Bracelet, by Angie Reano Owen, Santo Domingo Pueblo, ca. 1988; Bracelet, by Jesse Monongye, (Navajo/Hopi), ca. 1983. All from Indian Arts and Crafts Board Collection, Department of the Interior, at the National Museum of the American Indian, Smithsonian Institution.

The National Museum of the American Indian on the National Mall opened in 2004 as a major exhibition space as well as a center for performances, films, events, and educational activities. Designed in consultation with Native people, the sweeping curvilinear building represents the spirit of Native America on the nation's front lawn, and symbolizes the enduring presence of American Indians in contemporary life.

Opened in October 1994, the George Gustav Heye Center in lower Manhattan, in the heart of the financial district, serves as the National Museum of the American Indian's exhibition and education facility in New York City. Located in the Alexander Hamilton U.S. Custom House, one of the most splendid Beaux-Arts buildings in New York, the Heye Center features permanent and temporary exhibitions, as well as a range of public programs—including music and dance performances, films, and symposia—that explore the diversity of Native peoples and the strength and continuity of their cultures from earliest times to the present. The facility also includes a resource office where visitors can learn more about Native peoples, and a Film and Video Center, which houses a collection of recent works by independent and Native American filmmakers.

The Cultural Resources Center (CRC) is home to the museum's extensive collections and serves as a research facility for Native and non-Native scholars. Located just outside Washington, DC, in Suitland, Maryland, the CRC provides state-of-the-art resources and facilities for the conservation, handling, cataloging, and study of the museum's collections, library holdings, and photo and paper archives.

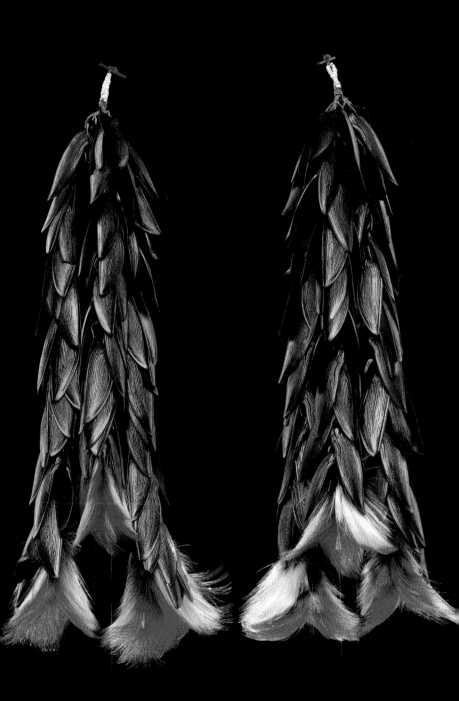

Navajo dolls, by Kay Bennett, Sheep Springs, New Mexico, ca. 1965. Indian Arts and Crafts Board Collection, Department of the Interior, at the National Museum of the American Indian, Smithsonian Institution.

COLLECTIONS

The collections of the former Museum of the American Indian, Heye Foundation, are the cornerstone of the National Museum of the American Indian. Assembled largely by wealthy New Yorker George Gustav Heye (1874–1957), the collections span more than 10,000 years of Native heritage in the U.S. (including Hawai'i), Canada, and Latin America. Among the thousands of masterworks are intricate wood, horn, and stone carvings from the Northwest Coast of North America; elegantly painted hides and garments from the Great Plains; pottery and basketry from the southwestern United States; ceramic figures from the Caribbean; jade carved by the Olmec and Maya peoples; textiles and gold offerings made by Andean cultures; elaborate featherwork by the peoples of Amazonia; and paintings and other works by contemporary Native American artists. About 70 percent of the 800,000 objects represent cultures in the United States and Canada; 30 percent represent cultures in Mexico and Central and South America.

THE NMAI ON THE NATIONAL MALL

The museum on the National Mall was designed by Douglas Cardinal (Blackfoot) and a team of Native architects and consultants to blend into the Mall's urban yet park-like setting, while retaining Native values. Natural features of the land, as well as the stone and masonry work of Chaco Canyon, Machu Picchu, and other Native sites, inspired the museum's designers to create a structure in which nature's rugged beauty and architecture's creative elegance come together in perfect harmony. The five-story, 250,000-square-foot, curvilinear building, clad in magnificent kasota limestone from Minnesota, evokes a natural rock formation swept by wind and water. Its dome, representative of the circular shapes in many Native cultures, complements the domed neoclassical buildings nearby.

The museum's grounds reflect the importance of Native peoples' connection have to the land. The landscape features four environments indigenous to the Chesapeake Bay region, including hardwood forest, wetlands, cropland, and meadow areas. Cardinal Direction Marker stones from Maryland, Canada, Hawai'i, and Chile stand with more than 40 large, uncarved rocks and boulders called Grandfather Rocks—reminders of the longevity of Native Americans' relationship to the natural world. The landscape also

Northern Cardinal Direction Marker outside the National Museum of the American Indian. The Tlicho (Dogrib) community of Behchoko, in Canada's Northwest Territories, blessed the stone before its journey to Washington, DC.

AT A GLANCE

Spanning the Western Hemisphere from the Arctic Circle to Tierra del Fuego, the collections of the National Museum of the American Indian are among the finest and most comprehensive assemblages of Native cultural materials in the world. Established by an Act of Congress in 1989, the museum works in collaboration with the indigenous peoples of the Western Hemisphere, including Hawai'i, to protect and foster cultures, reaffirm traditions and beliefs, encourage contemporary artistic expression, and provide a forum for Native perspectives.

includes a water feature, which begins as a powerful cascade tumbling over boulders at the northwest corner of the building. The water continues to flow beside the entry path, ending in a quiet pool beside the museum's main entrance.

The entrance to the National Museum of the American Indian on the National Mall faces east toward the rising sun. Just beyond the entrance extends the Potomac space, a circular gathering place for music, dance, cultural events, and tours. The Potomac—from an Algonquian-Powhatan word meaning "where the goods are brought in"—features a 120-foot-high atrium and eight large prism windows that, on sunny days, project a palette of brilliant rainbow colors throughout the space. An aerial sculpture entitled *Crux (as seen from those who sleep on the surface of the earth under the night sky)*, created by contemporary artist Brian Jungen, of Dunne-za First Nations ancestry, features five large animal figures— made from old and new luggage—that hang high above the floor.

The museum has several locations for Native presentations, drama, dance, music performances, demonstrations, readings, panel discussions, and seminars, including the 300-seat Rasmuson Theater (1st level). The Lelawi Theater (4th level) presents *Who We Are*, a 13-minute film that celebrates the vitality and diversity of Native life.

Exhibitions on the 2nd, 3rd, and 4th levels can be accessed from elevators located in the Potomac space. At the Resource Center (3rd level), visitors can find information about Native peoples as well as the museum's collections, and send an e-mail postcard to a friend. Other areas of interest include:

• The Mitsitam Native Foods Café (1st level), which serves meals and snacks based on the indigenous foods of the Americas.

• The Chesapeake Museum Store (1st level), which features jewelry, textiles, and other works by Native artisans.
• The Roanoke Museum Store (2nd level), offering a wide variety of merchandise, including books, crafts, music, souvenirs, and toys.

EXHIBITIONS

The National Museum of the American Indian on the National Mall presents diverse exhibitions, ranging from explorations of historical materials from the museum's vast collections to exhibitions of contemporary Native artistic expressions. Permanent exhibitions include *Our Universes: Traditional Knowledge Shapes Our World* (4th level); *Our Peoples: Giving Voice*

Above: East-facing entrance of the National Museum of the American Indian on the National Mall. Opposite: Klikitat Yakama Nation beaded bag, late 1800s.

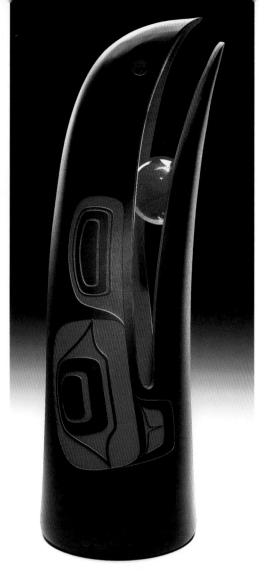

Raven Steals Sun,
by Preston Singletary
(Tlingit, b. 1963),
Seattle, Washington,
2003, blown and
sand-carved glass.

to Our Histories (4th level); Our Lives: Contemporary Lives and Identities (3rd level); Return to a Native Place: Algonquian Peoples of the Chesapeake (2nd level); and an introductory display near the museum's entrance that provides an overview of Native community, expression, encounter, and innovation. Window on Collections: Many Hands, Many Voices (3rd and 4th levels) showcases Native-made dolls, beadwork, containers, peace medals, arrowheads, and other objects. Beginning in October 2009, the W. Richard West, Jr., Changing Exhibitions Gallery (3rd level) will feature Strange Comfort, a major exhibition of the work of contempo-

Hattie Tom (Chiricahua, Apache), Omaha, Nebraska, ca. 1899.

rary mixed-media sculptor Brian Jungen, of Dunne-za First Nations ancestry. This will be followed in Fall 2010 by an exhibition of modern and contemporary works acquired by the museum during the previous seven years. The Sealaska Gallery (2nd level) will showcase a series of smaller exhibitions based on the museum's collections as well as changing contemporary exhibitions.

Exhibitions at the George Gustav Heye Center in New York City will include *A Song for the Horse Nation: Horses in Native American Cultures,* opening in November 2009, and *Infinity of Nations: History and Art in the Collections of the National Museum of the American Indian,* a major exhibition opening in October 2010 that showcases the cultural, historical, and geographic scope of the museum's holdings.

INFORMATION DESKS

The National Museum of the American Indian, Washington, DC: Visitor and membership information can be obtained at the Welcome Desk on the first level. Daily program information is also posted throughout the museum.

The George Gustav Heye Center, New York, NY: The information desk is located in the Great Hall, on the second floor across from the main museum entrance.

EDUCATIONAL PROGRAMS

A variety of interactive tours as well as special cultural presentations and films are offered for school groups. Reservations for these popular programs are required and should be made well in advance. To arrange a school group tour or program at the Mall museum, call 202-633-6644 or 888-618-0572, or email NMAI-Group-Reservations@si.edu. To arrange school group programs at the Heye Center, call 212-514-3705. For information about the full range of the museum's educational programs, visit our Web site at www.AmericanIndian.si.edu/education.

PUBLIC PROGRAMS

The National Museum of the American Indian (NMAI) provides opportunities for museum visitors to experience the living arts, cultures, and lifeways of the indigenous peoples of the Western Hemisphere and Hawai'i through performances, demonstrations, workshops, and the spoken word. For more information, please contact Cultural Arts staff at NMAIprograms@si.edu or visit our Web site at www.AmericanIndian.si.edu for a calendar of events.

MEMBERSHIP

To become an NMAI member and receive its full-color quarterly magazine *American Indian,* call 1-800-242-NMAI [6624] or click on Membership and Giving on the Web site.

RESOURCE CENTERS

The National Museum of the American Indian (NMAI) has Resource Centers in Washington, DC, and at the George Gustav Heye Center (GGHC) in New York City. In these open "library" areas, visitors can ask questions, explore DVDs, CD-ROMs, and Web sites, watch movies, handle objects, or research areas of interest. Both centers have a reference desk, study area, videos, hands-on collection

Above left: Maya polychrome vase, Nebaj, Guatemala, A.D. 550–850.
Opposite: Kwakwaka'wakw mechanical mask, late 19th c.

boxes, and an Interactive Learning Center, all of which are open to the public during museum hours.

Teachers and group leaders can make appointments to use the Resource Center at the Mall museum for special research projects and workshops. For information about the NMAI Resource Center in Washington, DC, call 202-633-6644.

Appointments can also be made to use the Heye Center's Haudenosaunee Discovery Room, a hands-on learning center for children. For information about Resource Center programs at the Heye Center, please call 212-514-3799.

FILM AND VIDEO

The Film and Video Center of the National Museum of the American Indian offers public presentations and information services about films, video, radio, television, and new media produced by and about the indigenous peoples of the Western Hemisphere. It organizes the NMAI's biennial Native American Film and Video Festival and screenings at the museum and in venues across the country. For information about film and video at the Heye Center, call 212-514-3737. For information about film and video at the National Museum of the American Indian in Washington, DC, call 202-633-6694.

MUSEUM AND GALLERY SHOPS

The National Museum of the American Indian in Washington, DC, has two stores. The Chesapeake Museum Store, on the museum's first level, features jewelry, textiles, and other works by Native artisans. The Roanoke Museum Store, on the museum's second level,

carries souvenirs and children's books and toys.

The Heye Center in New York has two stores. The Gallery Shop, featuring books and unique, handmade Indian jewelry and textiles, is located on the second floor near the main entrance. The Museum Store, with gifts, books, and toys related to Native American culture, is on the first floor.

MITSITAM NATIVE FOODS CAFÉ

The Mall museum's Zagat-rated café offers entrees, side dishes, snacks, desserts, and beverages based on the culinary traditions of five geographic regions covering the entire Western Hemisphere: Northern Woodlands, South America, Northwest Coast, Great Plains, and Mesoamerica. Named "Mitsitam," meaning "let's eat" in the Piscataway and Delaware languages, the popular café is the first museum dining facility to cover such a broad spectrum of Native foods and cultures.

Located on the musem's first level, across from the Rasmuson Theater, the Mitsitam Café is open from 10 A.M. to 5 P.M. The full menu is available from 11 A.M. to 3 P.M., with a smaller menu available from 3 P.M. to 5 P.M. daily.

Above: Frieze showing four scenes from the life of a Buddha, carved in high relief of seven pieces of dark gray-blue slate. Pakistan, Kushan dynasty (A.D. 50–200), late 2nd–early 3rd century A.D. Opposite: *White Avalokiteshvara*. Nepal, ca. 14th century, wood with pigment.

Independence Avenue
(accessible entrance)
at 12th Street, SW.
Mall entrance:
Jefferson Drive
at 12th Street, SW.
Open daily from
10 A.M. to 5:30 P.M.
Closed December 25.
Metrorail:
Smithsonian station.
Smithsonian
information:
202-633-1000
TTY: 202-633-5285.
asia.si.edu

FREER GALLERY OF ART

The Freer Gallery of Art opened in 1923 as the first national museum of fine arts. Its collection of Asian art is internationally preeminent. With works produced over six millennia, the Asian collections represent the creative traditions of China, Japan, Korea, South and Southeast Asia, and the West and includes examples of ancient Egyptian and early Christian art. Its select 19th- and early 20th-century American art boasts the world's largest and most important group of works by James McNeill Whistler (1834–1903). Because only a small part of the permanent collection can be shown at one time, changing selections of art are presented on a rotating schedule.

Charles Lang Freer (1854–1919), a Detroit industrialist, founded the museum; its unusual combination of creative tradi-

AT A GLANCE

The Freer Gallery of Art has one of the finest collections of Asian art in the world. These magnificent holdings, which span Neolithic times to the early 20th century, share exhibition space in the Italian Renaissance-style building with a major group of 19th- and early 20th-century American art. The Freer Gallery houses the world's most comprehensive collection of works by James McNeill Whistler, including *Harmony in Blue and Gold: The Peacock Room*, the artist's only existing interior design scheme, permanently installed in the Freer.

tions—Asian and American—reflect his unique preference. Freer began collecting American art in the 1880s. He limited his acquisitions to the work of a few living artists and concentrated especially on Whistler. He began collecting Asian art in 1887 and had assembled a collection of Asian masterpieces by the time of his death in 1919. Freer once wrote that he attempted to "gather together objects of art covering various periods of production, all of which are harmonious and allied in many ways."

In his bequest to the nation, Freer gave 7,500 Asian paintings, sculptures, and drawings, as well as works of calligraphy, metal, lacquer, and jade. Many other generous donors have since participated in the growth of the Asian collection, which now num-

bers 26,500 objects. Freer asked that his American collection remain as he presented it, with some 1,500 works by artists whom he knew personally and whose work he admired. The American collection has long been an inspiration for original research by scholars from many nations.

Freer also donated the funds for a building in which to house his collection. He believed the Italian Renaissance style would provide an appropriate setting for the display of his art, and he worked closely on the plans for the building with architect Charles A. Platt. The loggias, or open galleries that surround the gracious Italianate courtyard, enable visitors to enjoy views of beautiful plantings as well as bronze sculptures, which adorn the area. Today, the building is on the National Register of Historic Places. The Freer Gallery of Art is connected by an underground exhibition space to the Arthur M. Sackler Gallery, also a Smithsonian museum of Asian art.

Above: A detail of the northeast corner of *Harmony in Blue and Gold: The Peacock Room*, the only existing interior design scheme by James McNeill Whistler (American, 1834–1903) and an icon of the Freer Gallery of Art. Opposite top: Whistler's *Variations in Flesh Colour and Green: The Balcony*, 1864–70, oil on wood panel. Opposite bottom: Jar, Korea, Chosen period, Yi dynasty, ca. 1900, glazed porcelain clay.

Above: Katsushika Hokusai, *Boy Viewing Mount Fuji*, Japan, Edo period, ca. 1839, ink and color on silk. Right: Den Shiru (1743–1805), *Geomantic Verdit from the I-Ching*, hanging scroll, ink on paper. Opposite: The courtyard, Freer Gallery of Art.

Ongoing exhibitions include American art, Japanese art, Korean ceramics, Chinese painting, Whistler's *Harmony in Blue and Gold: The Peacock Room*, ancient Chinese art, Buddhist art, South Asian art, Islamic art, Egyptian glass, and "Luxury Arts of the Silk Route Empires." A variety of free public lectures, concerts, films, and other programs complement the exhibitions.

GENERAL INFORMATION

ENTRANCES

The main visitors' entrance is located on Jefferson Drive, SW. The street-level entrance on Independence Avenue has elevator service to the galleries. The Arthur M. Sackler Gallery is accessible through an underground gallery.

INFORMATION DESK

In the lobby near the Jefferson Drive entrance

TOURS

Free guided tours are offered daily, except Wednesdays and federal holidays. Tours are occasionally subject to cancellation; check with the information desk on the day of the tour or call 202-633-1000. Group tours are available with four week's advance registration. For more information or to schedule a tour, go to www.asia.si.edu, e-mail asiatours@si.edu, or call 202-633-1012 or 202-786-2374 (TTY).

GALLERY SHOP

Museum reproductions, books, posters, prints, jewelry, cards, and gifts related to the collections are for sale in the shop on the Freer's second level.

LIBRARY

A library serving the Freer and Sackler Galleries is located in the Sackler. It has 60,000-80,000 volumes, about half of which are in Chinese and Japanese, and subscribes to more than 400 periodicals. Library hours are 10 A.M. to 5 P.M., Monday through Friday. Please note the library and archives are located in the Sackler.

ARCHIVES

Researchers may examine the more than 100,000 historical photographic images in the archives, located in the Sackler. Appointments are necessary; call 202-633-0533.

Above: *Portrait of Yinti, Prince Xun, and Wife* (detail), China, Qing dynasty, 2d half 18th century, hanging scroll, ink and color on silk. Opposite top: Tomb guardian, China, Tang dynasty, 8th century, earthenware with lead glaze.

1050 Independence
Avenue, SW.
Entered from Enid A.
Haupt Garden through
ground-level pavilion.
Open daily from
10 A.M. to 5:30 P.M.
Closed December 25.
Metrorail:
Smithsonian station.
Smithsonian
information:
202-633-1000
TTY: 202-633-5285.
asia.si.edu

ARTHUR M. SACKLER GALLERY

Founded in 1987 with a group of 1,000 masterpieces of Asian art given by Arthur M. Sackler, M.D. (1913–1987), the Sackler Gallery is a leader in educating the public about a continent that plays an ever-larger role in the lives of Americans. The museum explores Asia's distinctive traditions in a varied program of exhibitions from its own collection and others in the United States and abroad. Archaeological riches lend variety to presentations from different centuries and geographic areas, including art, crafts, and design in many media.

Exhibitions of work by living artists have included such diverse examples as animal paintings by a young Chinese girl, baskets by an 80-year-old craftsman from rural Japan, installation art from a Chinese calligrapher, and a nine-foot-tall

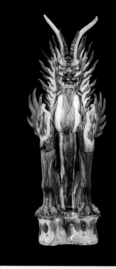

Album page, *A Demon Descends on a Horseman*, Iran, ca. 1550, opaque watercolor and gold on paper.

fiberglass work by an Indian sculptor. Some exhibitions and docent-led tours offer visitors the opportunity to touch objects and feel their weight and texture. A selection of porcelain masterworks by contemporary Japanese artists, for example, included pottery shards for visitors to handle. Reading areas furnished with educational materials are often incorporated into exhibition designs.

Programs of film, music, dance, and drama present a broad survey of Asian culture. Outdoor dance and

music perform- ances attract crowds to the art in- side. Members of local Asian communities often advise on and participate in the gallery's public programs. Regular public lectures reinforce themes introduced in the exhibitions or complement those topics with presentations of re- lated research.

Above: Sahiba Ram (1740–1800), frag- ment from a larger work showing Maharaja Pratap Singh with ladies of the royal harem, India, ca. late 18th century, opaque watercolor, silver, and gold on paper. Left: Rhyton, Iran, Sasanian period, A.D. 300–400, silver and gilt.

AT A GLANCE

The Arthur M. Sackler Gallery houses an important gift of Asian art from Arthur M. Sackler, M.D. (1913–1987). Exhibitions from the permanent collection as well as international presentations from Japan, China, Indonesia, Korea, India, Sri Lanka, and other nations trace the development of Asian and Near Eastern art from ancient times to the present.

The Sackler Gallery involves families through its popular "Imagin-Asia," a program of hands-on activities that encourage families to explore an exhibition and create a related project to take home. The workshops begin in the classroom on the second level. Themes and times vary and include weekends. For more information, call 202-633-0461.

Top: Shindo Susumu (b. 1952), bowl, Japan, 1992, porcelain with blue enamel glaze. Bottom: Two-headed bust, Jordan, ca. 6500 B.C.E., plaster and bitumen; lent by the Department of Antiquities of Jordan. Opposite: Raghubir Singh (b. 1942), *Men Exercise on the Sand Bank Facing Banaras*, photograph, India, 1986.

GENERAL INFORMATION

ENTRANCE

Enter from Independence Avenue through a ground-level pavilion and proceed to exhibition areas on two lower levels. The Freer Gallery of Art, with related exhibitions and programs, is accessible by an underground gallery.

INFORMATION DESK

In the entrance pavilion

TOURS

Free guided tours are offered daily, except Wednesdays and federal holidays. Tours are occasionally subject to cancellation; check with the Information Desk on the day of the tour or call 202-633-1000. Group tours are available with four week's advance registration. For more information or to schedule a tour go to www.asia.si.edu, e-mail asia tours@si.edu, or call 202-633-1012 or 202-786-2374 (TTY).

GALLERY SHOP

The shop, located on the first level, features merchandise based on the museum's collections and Asian cultures, including porcelain, crafts, jewelry, textiles, books, prints, and cards.

LIBRARY

A library serving the Freer and Sackler Galleries is located in the Sackler. It has 60,000-80,000 volumes, about half of which are in Chinese and Japanese, and subscribes to more than 400 periodicals. Library hours are 10 A.M. to 5 A.M., Monday through Friday.

ARCHIVES

Researchers may examine the more than 100,000 historical photographic images in the archives, located in the Sackler. Appointments are necessary; call 202-633-0533.

Face mask, Lele
peoples, Democratic
Republic of the Congo,
early to mid-20th century.
Opposite top: Headrest, Luba
peoples, Democratic Republic of
the Congo, mid to late 19th century.

950 Independence
Avenue, SW.
Entered from Enid A.
Haupt Garden through
ground-level pavilion.
Open daily from
10 A.M. to 5:30 P.M.
Closed December 25.
Metrorail:
Smithsonian station.
Smithsonian
information:
202-633-4690
TTY: 202-357-4814
africa.si.edu

NATIONAL MUSEUM OF AFRICAN ART

African art represents one of humanity's greatest achievements, fusing visual imagery with spiritual beliefs and social purpose. Its technical accomplishment and artistic perfection bear witness to the creative ingenuity of its makers. The National Museum of African Art's collections celebrate and explore the visual arts of the entire continent of Africa, from ancient to contemporary times. Through its collections, dynamic exhibitions, imaginative educational programs, and special collaborations with museums worldwide, the National Museum of African Art is raising the profile and importance of African art.

Right: Head, Edo peoples, Benin Kingdom, Nigeria, late 15th–early 16th century. Below: Crown, Yoruba peoples, Ijebu region, Nigeria, ca. 1930. Opposite top: Face mask, Chowke peoples, Democratic Republic of the Congo, early 20th century. Opposite bottom: Olowe of Ise (Nigerian, ca. 1875–1938), Yoruba peoples, *Bowl with Figures*, ca. 1925.

EXHIBITIONS

To build in-depth understanding of cultures in which art and life are one, the National Museum of African Art's exhibitions present the finest examples of sculpture and masks, architectural elements, utilitarian objects, textiles, objects of adornment, archival photographs, and contemporary art in all media. The museum's collections are regularly rotated throughout its exhibitions. The National Museum of African Art acquired the Walt Disney-Tishman African Art Collection, which contains 525 works of art. A permanent space devoted to the collection houses a selection of these objects. Two changing galleries include the Sylvia H. Williams Gallery for contemporary African art and the second-level gallery. Also on the second level are a lecture hall, an educational workshop, a library, and the Eliot Elisofon Photographic Archives.

PUBLIC PROGRAMS

More than 30 million Americans trace their heritage to the cultures and traditions of Africa. With a variety of programs and resources for people of all ages, the museum is a portal to African arts and culture. It offers guided tours, hands-on workshops, storytelling, scholarly symposia, music and dance programs, films, teacher training workshops, audiovisual loan programs, and much more. "Let's Read About Africa," a program for young people ages 5-10, introduces young audiences to current and classical children's literature about Africa. Each reading is followed by a discussion, demonstration, or art activity. Information about public programs and exhibitions is published in the museum's calendar and is available at

151

Right: Garth Erasmus
(b. 1956), *The Muse #3*,
1995.
Below: Magdalene
Anyango N. Odundo
(b. 1950), *Untitled #1*,
1994.
Opposite: Constance
Larrabee (1915–2000),
Zulu Girl and Children,
near Ixopo, Natal, South
Africa, 1949.

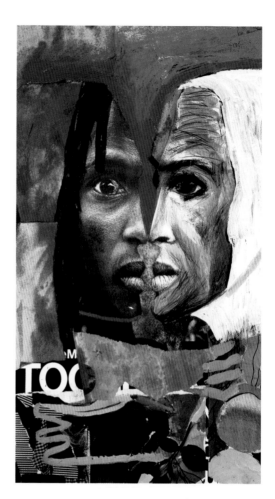

the museum's Web site, africa.si.edu. To receive the
calendar, write to: Calendar, National Museum of
African Art, Smithsonian Institution, PO Box 37012,
Washington, DC 20560-0708.

Studio Africa, an outreach program for young audiences, creates a comprehensive learning environment
for young people by exploring the art and cultures of
Africa through monthly classroom workshops and
demonstrations.

RESEARCH FACILITIES

The National Museum of African Art is a leading research and reference center for the arts of Africa. The
Eliot Elisofon Photographic Archives, with 300,000

photographic prints and transparencies, extensive unedited film footage, and videos and documentary films on African art, specializes in the collection and preservation of visual materials on African art, culture, and the environment. The hours are from 10 A.M. to 4 P.M., Monday through Friday, by appointment; call 202-633-4690. The Warren M. Robbins Library, named for the museum's founder, contains more than 32,000 volumes on African art and material culture. The library is open from 9 A.M. to 5:15 P.M., Monday through Friday, by appointment; call 202-633-4680.

GENERAL INFORMATION

INFORMATION DESK

In the entrance pavilion

TOURS

Museum tours are offered for individuals on a walk-in basis at select times. Tours for school and community groups are available by appointment. To request a tour schedule or to make an appointment, call 202-633-4646, or 202-357-4814 (TTY).

MUSEUM STORE

African jewelry, textiles, sculpture, musical recordings, books, exhibition catalogues, posters, and postcards are for sale.

Above: The north side of the Arts and Industries Building with the Kathrine Dulin Folger

900 Jefferson Drive, SW
(next to the
Smithsonian Castle).
Closed for renovation.
Metrorail:
Smithsonian station.
Smithsonian
information:
202-633-1000
TTY: 202-633-5285.
www.si.edu/ai

ARTS AND INDUSTRIES BUILDING

If you could step into the Arts and Industries Building, located just east of the Castle, you'd be transported back to 1881. The building opened that year in time for President James Garfield's Inaugural Ball. Over the years, the Arts and Industries Building has housed and shown many popular objects and exhibitions, from the First Ladies' gowns to the *Spirit of St. Louis* and to the long-running "1876: A Centennial Exhibition."

The three main halls of the Arts and Industries Building has hosted a variety of large-scale changing exhibitions on art, history, science, and culture. The building is currently closed in preparation for renovation.

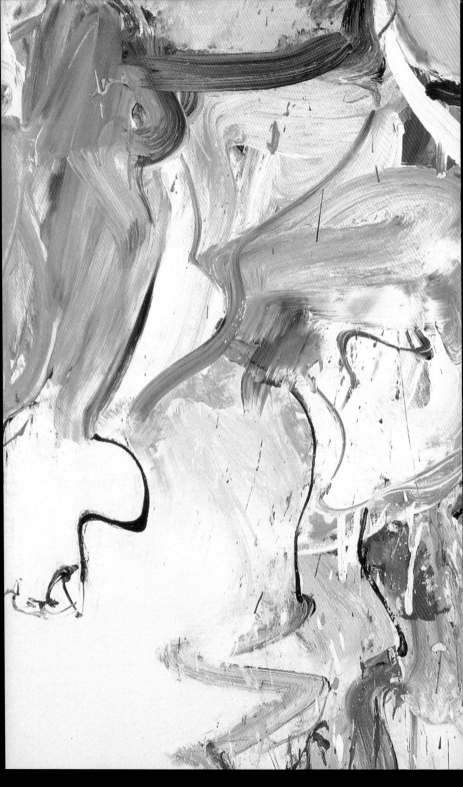

Above: Willem de Kooning (1904–1997), *Woman, Sag Harbor* (detail), 1964. Opposite top:

Claes Oldenburg (b. 1929), *7-Up*, 1961.

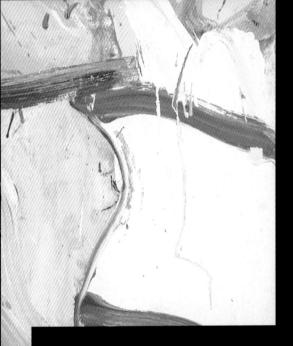

HIRSHHORN MUSEUM AND SCULPTURE GARDEN

Independence Avenue at 7th Street, SW. Building and Plaza entered from Independence Avenue; Plaza and Sculpture Garden entered from National Mall. Open daily. Building, 10 A.M. to 5:30 P.M.; Plaza, 7:30 A.M. to 5:30 P.M.; Sculpture Garden, 7:30 A.M. to dusk. Closed December 25. Metrorail: L'Enfant Plaza station. Smithsonian information: 202-633-1000 TTY: 202-357-1729. www.hirshhorn.si.edu

This strikingly designed museum of modern and contemporary art is named after the dedicated and enthusiastic American art collector Joseph H. Hirshhorn (1899–1981). His gifts and bequest to the nation of more than 12,000 works are the nucleus of a dynamic collection that remains current through purchases and gifts from many donors. When the museum opened in 1974, the Smithsonian offered, for the first time, a history of modern art in a building and sunken garden that were bold, even daring, by contemporary architectural standards.

Today, the museum is for many the most challenging and visually stimulating of the Institution's attractions on the National Mall. Museum-goers may be dazzled or perplexed by what is on view.

Top: David Smith (1906–1965), *Cubi XII*, 1963.
Above: Mark di Suvero (b. 1933), *Are Years What? (for Marianne Moore)*, 1967.
Right: Constantin Brancusi (1876–1957), *Torso of a Young Man*, 1924.

but the experience is seldom boring. Art, especially new art, can evoke powerful responses.

A PLACE FOR SCULPTURE . . .

Sculpture was a special passion of the museum's founding donor, and the Hirshhorn's sculpture collection is one of the most distinguished in the world. Sculptures by international artists can be seen throughout the museum, alongside the paintings or in mini-surveys along window walls overlooking the fountain, as well as amid the greenery of the outdoor fountain plaza and along pathways of the Garden. There, adjacent to the National Mall, are several signature works: Auguste Rodin's figure ensemble, *Monument to the Burghers of Calais* of 1884–89; compositions by mid-century sculptural giants Henry Moore and David Smith; and the definitive, soaring red steel construction by Mark di Suvero, *Are Years What? (for Marianne Moore)*, 1967, to name a few. Closer to the museum itself, contemporary sculpture is the keynote: here, with the building hovering above, are Juan Muñoz's bronze figures resembling ventriloquists' dummies, *Last Conversation Piece,* 1994–95, and Tony Smith's minimal yet intricate *Throwback,* 1976–79, among others.

. . . AND THE ART OF OUR TIME

Joseph Hirshhorn was dedicated to the art and artists of his time. As he tended to purchase many pieces by artists he particularly admired, the museum is able to present in-depth explorations of such groundbreaking figures as Alexander Calder, Willem de Kooning, and Clyfford Still.

Continuing in Joseph Hirshhorn's tradition, the museum remains committed to acquiring and exhibiting work by emerging and established contemporary artists. Recent acquisition galleries feature the latest pieces to enter the collection and have included

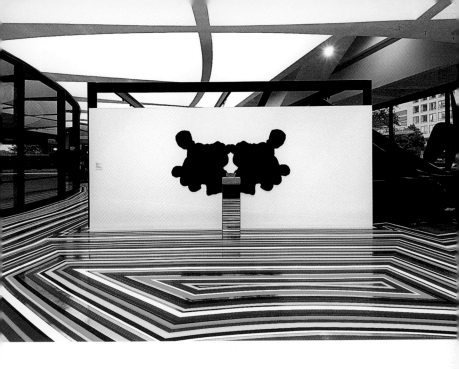

Jim Lambie (b. 1964), *Zobop*, 2006. Installation view of *Directions: Jim Lambie* in the museum's entrance, 2006.

such visitor favorites as Ann Hamilton's intriguing installation containing beeswax tablets and live snails, *palimpsest*, 1989, and Ron Mueck's *Untitled (Big Man)*, 2000.

The museum's Black Box, which screens works by artists and filmmakers from around the world, highlights the growing importance of film and video as an artistic medium. The *Directions* series, which since 1987 has featured the work of emerging artists, has ranged in scope from gallery installations to interventions both within and on the building to performance pieces involving members of the community. Partnering with artists in all aspects of its programming is an important part of the Hirshhorn's mission, so the museum has created *Ways of Seeing*, an ongoing exhibition project that invites noted artists, filmmakers, authors, and others to explore the collection and create installations that express their own unique perspectives and visions.

Rotating collection exhibitions on all levels of the museum demonstrate the diversity of styles, subjects, and media pursued by an international mix of artists, and have focused on such concepts as sculptors and their drawings, form and formlessness, and repetition

Above: Chuck Close
(b. 1940), *Roy II,* 1994.
Opposite: Georgia
O'Keeffe (1887–1986),
Goat's Horn with Red,
1945.

of materials and imagery. In addition, important mono-graphic and thematic special exhibitions fill the second-level galleries. This dynamic array of presentations of-fers fresh contexts for exploring modern and contemporary art as well as new ways of looking at the museum's diverse holdings. The galleries on each level continually present a blend of familiar masterpieces and innovative recent works that are sure to intrigue and en-gage both newcomers and frequent visitors to the Hir-shhorn.

LOOK, LEARN, CREATE

The Hirshhorn offers a range of educational experiences for young and old alike, including lectures and tours by artists and curators, independent film series, informative docent-led tours of the permanent collection, and an array of programs, workshops, and activities. For families, there are interactive events such as the Artist at Work with Youth program, in which artists conduct creative projects with children to foster their discovery of the museum and explore ideas about art. The ArtLab for Teens workshops connect youth with local artists to investigate current exhibitions at the museum through art-making. The mu-

seum also collaborates with teachers and students to plan tours and activities that meet curriculum goals. Additionally, Interpretive Guides, who are students and young art professionals, interact with visitors in the galleries to answer questions and discuss the exhibitions.

The popular Meet the Artist series, begun in 2000, brings notable artists from around the world to Washington for lectures and discussions about their creative process and recent work. Speakers have included

As the Smithsonian's showcase for modern and contemporary art, the Hirshhorn Museum and Sculpture Garden provides a comprehensive look at art from the first stirrings of modernism in the 19th century to the most recent developments in the art world. Sculpture by modern masters (much of it situated outdoors), international modernist works of the postwar era, and contemporary art are particular attractions. American and European Cubism, Social Realism, Surrealism, Geometric Abstraction, and Expressionism trace modern art past the mid-20th century. Contemporary currents range from Pop art of the 1960s to recent explorations by emerging artists working in a variety of media.

such influential figures as Marina Abramovic, John Baldessari, Matthew Barney, Ernesto Neto, Lorna Simpson, and Hiroshi Sugimoto. Friday lunchtime talks by artists and staff members provide informal

occasions to learn more about the collection as well as exhibitions. In Conversation talks give visitors the rare opportunity to learn about works in the galleries from the artists themselves or to experience the collection from an artist's perspective, while museum staff offer focused explorations of individual pieces on view.

Opposite: Ron Mueck (b. 1958), *Untitled (Big Man)*, 2000.
Above: Dana Hoey (b. 1966), *Waimea*, 2000.

A BOLD SETTING

Gordon Bunshaft (1909–1990), winner in 1987 of the Pritzker Prize in architecture, designed the Hirshhorn. Redesigns of the Sculpture Garden in 1981 and the Plaza in 1993 increased accessibility and enhanced the placement of sculpture with additional greenery. The dynamic and unorthodox building—82 feet high and 231 feet in diameter—encircles an open courtyard and an asymmetrically placed bronze fountain. The exterior wall is a solid surface, broken only by a window 70 feet long in the third-level Abram Lerner Room, from which visitors may enjoy a spectacular view of the National Mall. Floor-to-ceiling windows define the inner

Above: Andy Warhol
(1928–1987),
Self-Portrait, 1986.
© The Andy Warhol
Foundation for the Visual
Arts/ARS, New York.
Right: Stephan Balkenhol
(b.1957), *Three Hybrids*,
1995.
Opposite top: Richard
Diebenkorn (1922–1993),
*Man and Woman in a Large
Room*, 1957.
Opposite bottom:
Robert Gober (b. 1954),
Untitled, 1990.

core, which overlooks the fountain. Four massive piers elevate the concrete structure above the walled plaza. The recessed garden across Jefferson Drive, with its rectangular reflecting pool, provides a peaceful area for viewing art. Outdoors at the Hirshhorn, benches, shaded areas, and fountainside tables provide attractive spots in which to linger. Please enjoy— but do not touch the sculpture!

GENERAL INFORMATION

INFORMATION DESK

Located in the lobby and staffed from
10 A.M. to 4 P.M. daily. Information
about exhibitions and events is
available here.

TOURS

Docent-led tours of the permanent collection are offered upon request and
Interpretive Guides are available for

discussions in the galleries daily
between noon and 4 P.M. Tours for groups
with up to 60 participants can be scheduled with four weeks' advance notice.
Tours of the Sculpture Garden are
available June through October and other
times upon request, weather permitting.
The Programs Department offers tours
in French, Spanish, and German upon
request. Sign-language tours in the
Sculpture Garden for visitors who are
blind or have limited vision are also
available with advance scheduling.
To contact the department for further
information call 202-633-EDUC (3382).

PUBLIC PROGRAMS

A variety of free films, lectures,
symposia, and talks by artists are
presented regularly in the Marion and
Gustave Ring Auditorium on the lower
level. Other programs include gallery
talks, workshops for a variety of audiences, family art activities, summer
music concerts, and programs for teachers, schools, and community groups. For
information, call 202-633-EDUC (3382).

MUSEUM STORE

The museum store offers exhibition
catalogues, postcards, books on art,
and other items related to the museum's programs.

Above: Sorting mail on moving trains, which began after the Civil War, was one of the postal service's great innovations. Opposite top: This badge was worn by a pilot in the Airmail Service, which was in operation from August 12, 1918, to September 1, 1927, during which time more than 6,500 planes were forced to land and 32 pilots died flying.

2 Massachusetts
Avenue at First
Street, NE
(in the Washington
City Post Office
Building next to
Union Station).
Open daily from
10 A.M. to 5:30 P.M.
Closed December 25.
Metrorail:
Union Station.
Information:
202-633-5550
TTY: 202-633-9849.
postal museum.si.edu

NATIONAL POSTAL MUSEUM

We are a migratory people. Our brothers, our neighbors, our children go away from us and the means of communication with them by letter and newspapers is one of the strongest ties that binds [*sic*] us together.

Congressman Horace Maynard,
Tennessee, 1859

Mail touches everyone, making the boundaries of postal history limitless. America's postal history can be defined through the use of objects as small as stamps and as mammoth as airplanes. It is expressed in heartrending letters from soldiers on foreign battlefields and through the explosion of direct-mail marketing. America's postal service was the force behind the creation of commercial aviation. It helped push the development of cross-country stagecoach routes

and railroads. It ensured the development and perpetual maintenance of rural roads. The postal service was where thousands of African Americans were first able to obtain government employment. America's postal history is the story of the people who made the service work and those who used it. It is the history of mail and the American people.

The National Postal Museum opened on July 30, 1993. Located on Capitol Hill, the museum is housed in the old City Post Office Building. The building, designed by Daniel Burnham, was built between 1911 and 1914. It is a classic Beaux Arts-style structure that complements its next-door neighbor, the Burnham-designed Union Station. The museum has 23,000 square feet of exhibition space, a research library, a stamp store, and a museum store.

The ornate historic lobby formerly served as the main service area of the City Post Office Building. By the 1970s that part of the building had been modernized to an unrecognizable point, a hodge-podge of Formica™ and harsh fluorescent lighting. Painstaking renovation begun in 1989 restored every foot of the lobby to its original grandeur. Today, the lobby is the foyer to the National Postal Museum.

BINDING THE NATION

This gallery traces events from colonial times through the 19th century, stressing the importance of written communication in the development of the new nation.

As early as 1673, regular mail was carried between New York and Boston following Indian trails. As co-deputy postmaster for the colonies, Benjamin Franklin played a key role in establishing mail service. After the Revolution, Americans recognized that the postal service, and the news and information it carried, was essential to binding the nation together. By 1800, mail was carried over more than 9,000 miles of postal roads. The challenge of developing mail service over long distances is the central theme of "The Expanding Nation," which chronicles the creation of the Butterfield Overland Mail stagecoach line and the famed Pony Express. An interactive video station invites visitors to create their own postal routes.

Above: Children especially enjoy climbing aboard a replica of a 19th-century mudwagon, a Western-style stagecoach.
Opposite: Revenue stamps were first issued in 1862 and continued after the war. In the early 1870s, they ranged in denomination from one cent to $5,000, like this example, which was approved but never issued.

Above: Concord coaches, such as this one from 1851, could hold up to twelve passengers and the mail. Opposite top: This handstamp was salvaged from the U.S.S. *Oklahoma*, which sank at Pearl Harbor in 1941. Opposite bottom: Eddie Gardner wore this helmet when flying for the Airmail Service in 1918 for protection in the open cockpits.

CUSTOMERS AND COMMUNITIES

By the turn of the 20th century the nation's population was expanding, as was mail volume and the need for personal mail delivery. Crowded cities and the requirements of rural Americans inspired the invention of new delivery methods. Facets of the developing system and its important role in the fabric of the nation are explored using photographs, mail vehicles, a variety of rural mailboxes, and other artifacts.

Parcel Post Service helped usher in an era of consumerism by the early 20th century that foreshadowed the massive mechanization and automation of mail and the mail-order industry. Today, mail service is a vital conduit for business. In the "What's in the Mail for You!" gallery, visitors can create graphic profiles of themselves as a target market for direct mailers.

MOVING THE MAIL

Faced with the challenge of moving the mail quickly, the postal service was constantly on the lookout for the fastest transportation system available, from post riders to stagecoaches, automobiles and trucks, to trains and airplanes. These various means of transportation are the focus of the museum's atrium gallery.

"Moving the Mail" features three vintage airmail planes, a 1931 Ford Model A postal truck, an 1851 stagecoach, a replica of a railway mail car, and a full-size semi truck cab cutaway.

After the Civil War, postal officials began to take advantage of trains for moving and sorting the mail. Railway mail clerks worked the mail while it was being carried between towns. In 1918, airmail service was established on a regular basis between New York, Philadelphia, and Washington, DC. Airmail contracts provided funding for the development of the commercial aviation industry.

Visitors will discover the story of Owney, a little stray dog adopted by postal workers in New York. He became the mascot of the Railway Mail Service and traveled thousands of miles across the United States.

THE ART OF CARDS AND LETTERS

Personal letters are vivid windows into history. A series of changing exhibits in this gallery conveys the stories of families and friends who are bound together by letters over distance and across time. A poignant video is the highlight of "Mail Call," an exhibit celebrating the bond of

Above: Stamps and other philatelic materials form the core of the museum's collections. Opposite: The Post Office Department promoted its speedy new service with posters in post offices across the country.

mail between soldiers and their loved ones back home.

THE PHILATELIC GALLERY

Since Great Britain issued the first adhesive postal stamp in 1840, stamps of every subject, shape, and design have been produced for consumer use or as collectibles. Stamps not only serve as proof of postage. They are also miniature works of art, keepsakes, rare treasures, and the workhorses of the automated postal system. Some stamps tell stories, while others contain secrets and hidden meanings.

Stamps from the United States and around the world are on display in the museum's pull-out frames. Featuring stamps from the museum's vast collection as well as special items from other collections, the gallery offers visitors access to spectacular rarities. Changing philatelic exhibits have featured Franklin D. Roosevelt's stamp sketches, the first U.S. stamps, and the 24-cent inverted Jenny airmail stamp of 1918, possibly the most famous U.S. stamp.

GENERAL INFORMATION

ENTRANCE

Enter the lobby of the building and proceed by escalator to the floor level of the museum's 90-foot-high atrium.

INFORMATION DESK

Off the lobby

TOURS

Scheduled tours for students and groups of 10 or more are available. Reservations for these tours must be made three weeks in advance. For a walk-in tour schedule, or to make reservations for a student or group tour, call 202.633.5535 or 202.633.9849 (TTY).

PUBLIC PROGRAMS

An array of public programs offer visitors fresh perspectives on mail in their lives. Museum programs include hands-on workshops, interactive family programs, films, lectures, performances, and much more. Sign language and oral interpreters for programs and tours require two weeks' advance notice. For more information about upcoming public programs, call 202.633.5533 or visit the museum's Web site.

RESEARCH FACILITIES

With more than 40,000 volumes and manuscripts, the museum's library is among the world's largest facilities for postal history and philatelic research. The library features a specimen study room, an audiovisual viewing room, and a rare book collection. Open by appointment, Monday through Friday from 10 A.M. to 4 P.M.; call 202-633-9370 to schedule a visit.

MUSEUM STORE

Located near the escalators at the museum entrance, the museum store offers posters, T-shirts, stationery, postcards, pins, first-day covers, stamp-collector kits, stamp- and postal-related souvenirs, books for all ages on postal-history subjects and letter collections, and a selection of philatelic publications.

STAMP STORE

Operated by the US Postal Service, the stamp store is located opposite the museum store. Visitors may purchase a variety of current stamps and other commemorative stamp items.

US POST OFFICE

Accessible from the main hall of the museum.

The Donald W. Reynolds Center for American Art and Portraiture is home to the
National Portrait Gallery and the Smithsonian American Art Museum. Opposite left:
Stuart Davis (1894-1964), *Int'l Surface No. 1*, 1960. Smithsonian American Art Museum.
Opposite right: Tom Wolfe (b. 1931) by Everett Raymond Kinstler, 2000, oil on canvas.
National Portrait Gallery; gift of Sheila Wolfe. © 2002 Everett Raymond Kinstler.

DONALD W. REYNOLDS CENTER FOR AMERIC

ART AND PORTRAITURE

The National Portrait Gallery and the Smithsonian American Art Museum
located in the heart of downtown Washington, DC. Their recently renova
National Historic Landmark building is a dazzling showcase for American
and portraiture that celebrates the vision and creativity of Americans. The
museums share a main entrance at 8th and F Streets NW, which provides
access to current information on special exhibitions, public programs, anc
visitor amenities.

The museums and their specialized new facilities—the Lunder Conserv
Center, the Luce Foundation Center for American Art, the Nan Tucker Mc
Auditorium, and the Robert and Arlene Kogod Courtyard—are now knov
collectively as the Donald W. Reynolds Center for American Art and Portr

Robert and Arlene Kogod Courtyard
The Robert and Arlene Kogod Courtyard is enclosed with an elegant glas
canopy, a signature element shared by the two museums. It was designed
world-renowned architects Foster + Partners and provides a distinctive, c
porary accent to the museums' Greek Revival building.

Lunder Conservation Center
The museums share the innovative Lunder Conservation Center, the first
conservation facility with floor-to-ceiling glass windows that allow the pu
permanent behind-the-scenes views of the museums' preservation work.
tors can learn about conservation science through educational kiosks, vic
and public programs.

Above: M. F. K. Fisher (1908–1992) by Ginny Stanford, acrylic on canvas (detail), 1991.
© Ginny Stanford. Opposite top: Benjamin Harrison (1833–1901) by an unidentified artist,
1888, wood. Opposite, bottom: Barack Obama (b. 1961) by Shepard Fairey. Gift of the
Heather and Tony Podesta Collection. © She and Fairey (Obey Give)

8th and F Streets, NW.
Open daily from
11:30 A.M. to 7 P.M.
Closed December 25.
Metrorail:
Gallery
Place/Chinatown
Museum information:
202-633-8300.
Smithsonian
information:
202-633-1000
TTY: 202-633-5285.
www.npg.si.edu

NATIONAL PORTRAIT GALLERY

Generations of remarkable Americans are kept in the good company of their fellow citizens at the National Portrait Gallery. The museum presents the wonderful diversity of individuals who have left and who are still leaving their mark on our country and our culture. Through the visual and performing arts, we feature leaders such as George Washington and Martin Luther King Jr., artists such as Mary Cassatt and George Gershwin, activists such as Sequoyah and Rosa Parks, and icons of pop culture such as Babe Ruth and Marilyn Monroe, among thousands of others. They all link us to our past, our present, and our future. For anyone fascinated by famous Americans and their stories, the National Portrait

HOPE

The Portrait Gallery reopened in 2006 after an extensive six-year renovation of its National Historic Landmark building. The structure itself, begun in 1836 for the US Patent Office, stood for the highest aspirations of the nation. Praised by Walt Whitman as "the noblest of Washington buildings," it was saved from the wrecking ball in 1958 and then welcomed the opening of the National Portrait Gallery in 1968. That was no accident. Pierre L'Enfant, in his design for the new federal city, had envisioned for this site a place to honor the nation's heroes. In our own time, a building has been reborn and a vision fulfilled.

Portraiture as an art form is alive across the United States. In several exhibitions each year, the National Portrait Gallery showcases new talent and new faces. Every three years, the Outwin Boochever Portrait

Competition invites artists to submit their work to be considered for entrance into the exhibition, cash prizes, and the top prize of executing a commission of a remarkable living American for the museum. And in "Portraiture Now," the museum continues a new series of exhibitions featuring contemporary artists who explore with imagination and skill the age-old art of depicting the figure. Through paintings, sculpture, photographs, drawings, and video art, these artists bring compelling figurative art into the twenty-first century.

One of the building's most popular exhibitions is "America's Presidents," the nation's only complete collection of presidential portraits outside of the White House. This exhibition lies at the heart of the Portrait Gallery's mission to tell the country's history through the individuals who have shaped it. Visitors can see an enhanced and extended display of

United States, including Gilbert Stuart's "Lansdowne" portrait of George Washington, the famous "cracked plate" photograph of Abraham Lincoln, and whimsical sculptures of Lyndon Johnson, Jimmy Carter, Richard Nixon, and George H. W. Bush by noted caricaturist

Faith Ringgold (b. 1930) *Self-portrait from 7 Passages to a Flight*, 1998, quilt with hand-painted etching. Faith Ringgold © 1998.

Pat Oliphant. Presidents Washington, Andrew Jackson, Lincoln, Theodore Roosevelt, and Franklin D. Roosevelt are given expanded attention because of their significant impact on the office.

A "conversation about America" is on view in a series of seventeen galleries and alcoves entitled "American Origins," which is chronologically arranged to take the visitor from the days of first contact between Native Americans and European explorers, through the struggles of independence, to the Gilded Age. Major figures include Pocahontas, Alexander Hamilton, Henry Clay, Nathaniel Hawthorne, and Harriet Beecher Stowe.

Three galleries devoted to the Civil War—"Faces of Discord"—examine this conflict in depth. A selection of modern photographic prints produced from Mathew Brady's original negatives complements the exhibition. Highlights from the Gallery's remarkable collection of daguerreotypes (the earliest practical form of photography) make the National Portrait Gallery the first major museum to create a permanent exhibition space for daguerreotype portraits.

Each year, a gallery within the museum called "One Life" is devoted to a single curator's exploration of the life of an individual.

Four newly created galleries opening onto the museum's magnificent third-floor Great Hall showcase the major cultural, scientific, and political figures of the 20th century, including cultural icon Marilyn Monroe. From the reform movements of the first two decades to the movements for social justice and civil rights of the 1950s, 1960s, and 1970s, and from the Great Depression to the Vietnam era and beyond, visitors can experience the people who defined the decades of the 20th century.

Fred Astaire (1899-1987) by Edward Steichen, 1927, gelatin silver print. Acquired in memory of Agnes and Eugene Meyer through the generosity of Katharine Graham and the New York Community Trust, The Island Fund. Permisssion of Joanna T. Steichen © The Estate of Edward Steichen.

Two exhibitions on the third-floor mezzanines feature particular themes in American life. "Bravo!" features individuals who have brought the performing arts to life, from the late 19th century through the present. "Champions" salutes the dynamic American sports figures whose impact has extended beyond

AT A GLANCE

Through the visual, performing, literary, and electronic arts, the National Portrait Gallery provides a stage for remarkable Americans to share their stories with us. Highlights from the Gallery's collections include Gilbert Stuart's "Lansdowne" painting of George Washington, perhaps the most significant portrait in America's history, as well as exhibitions on the presidents, paintings, photographs, and drawings. In addition to its popular Web site, the Gallery has produced "Civil War@Smithsonian" highlighting the Smithsonian's Civil War collections.

John Brown (1800–1859) by Augustus Washington, ca. 1846–47, daguerreotype. Purchased with major acquisition funds and with funds donated by Betty Adler Schermer in honor of her great-grandfather, August M. Bondi.

the athletic realm and made them a part of the larger story of the nation. A lively combination of portraits, artifacts, memorabilia, and videos enhances both exhibitions.

There are several ways to connect with the National Portrait Gallery's collections and programs if you are unable to visit in person. The Portrait Gallery's Web site, one of the most visited among Smithsonian

museums' sites, allows users to experience a virtual visit to current—and many past—exhibitions. Visitors may also search for records of portraits in the museum's collection, as well as those identified in other collections by the Catalog of American Portraits. Additionally, the museum's blog, *Face-to-Face*, provides behind-the-scenes stories and in-depth profiles of artists and sitters. It is an online element of public programming for the museum. The museum has not, of course, abandoned the printed page, and takes pride in the many books associated with its exhibitions.

The National Portrait Gallery's education department uses art as a vehicle to introduce individuals in the museum's collection, along with their significant contributions to American society. The department develops innovating thoughtful programming for visitors from near and far. Using the exhibitions in the museum as a catalyst for these educational offerings the department brings the collection alive through interactive school tours, docent tours, and programming.

Rosa Parks (1913–2005) by Marshall D. Rumbaugh, 1983, limewood.

Above: Edward Hopper (1882-1967), Cape Cod Morning (detail), 1950, oil on canvas.

Opposite top: Roy Lichtenstein, (1923-1977) *Modern Head*, 1974/1990, painted

stainless steel © Estate of Roy Lichtenstein. Opposite bottom: *Childe Hassam*

(1859-1935) The South Ledges, Appledore, 1913, oil on canvas.

8th and F Streets, NW
Open daily from
11:30 A.M. to 7 P.M.
Closed December 25.
Metrorail:
Gallery Place /
Chinatown station
Museum information:
202-275-1500
(recorded)
202-633-7970
www.AmericanArt.si.edu

Smithsonian
information:
202-633-1000
TTY: 202-633-5285

SMITHSONIAN

AMERICAN

ART MUSEUM

The Smithsonian American Art Museum,
the nation's first collection of American
art, is an unparalleled record of the
American experience. The collection
captures the aspirations, character, and
imagination of the American people over
three centuries.

More than 7,000 artists are represented
in the museum's collection, including
masters such as John Singleton Copley,
Winslow Homer, John Singer Sargent,
Mary Cassatt, Georgia O'Keeffe, Edward
Hopper, Jacob Lawrence, David Hockney,
Lee Friedlander, Nam June Paik, Martin
Puryear, and Robert Rauschenberg.
Artworks in the collection reveal key
aspects of America's rich artistic and
cultural history from the colonial period

Georgia O'Keeffe (1887–1986), *Manhattan*, 1932, oil on canvas. Gift of the Georgia O'Keeffe Foundation.

The museum's historic Greek Revival building has been meticulously renovated with expanded permanent collection galleries and the new Luce Foundation Center for American Art, the first visible art storage and study center in Washington.

The museum has been a leader in collecting and exhibiting works of art. Pioneering collections include historic and contemporary folk art; work by African American and Latino artists; photography from its origins in the 19th century to contemporary works; images of western expansion; and realist art from the first half of the 20th century. The museum has the largest collection of New Deal art and murals, and the largest collection of American sculpture

LUCE FOUNDATION CENTER FOR AMERICAN ART

The Luce Foundation Center, the first visible art study and storage center in Washington, provides new ways to experience American art with more than 3,300 artworks from the museum's collection on display. It features paintings densely hung on screens; sculptures, craft and folk art objects arranged on shelves; and portrait miniatures, bronze medals and jewelry in drawers that slide open with the touch of a button. Interpretive materials and artist biographies are available for every work.

As a major center for research in American art, the museum includes such resources as the Inventory of American Paintings executed before 1914, with data on nearly 290,000 works; the Peter A. Juley & Sons collection of 127,000 historic photographs; the Pre-1877 Art Exhibition Catalogue Index; the Inventory of American Sculpture, with information on more than 85,000 indoor and outdoor works; and the Joseph Cornell Study Center.

Albert Pinkham Ryder (1847–1917), *Flying Dutchman,* **1887, oil on canvas mounted on fiberboard.**

John Singer Sargent
(1856–1925), *Elizabeth
Winthrop Chanler*, 1893,
oil on canvas. Opposite
above: Nam June Paik
(1932– 2006), *Electronic
Super-highway: Conti-
nental U.S., Alaska, Hawaii*,
(detail) 1995, 49-channel
closed circuit video
installation, neon, steel,
and electronic compo-
nents. © Nam June Paik.
Opposite: George Catlin
(1796–1872), *Buffalo
Bull's Back Fat, Head
chief, Blood Tribe*, 1832,
oil on canvas.

COLLECTIONS

The Smithsonian American Art Museum's collection
tells the story of America through the visual arts.
Colonial portraiture, 19th-century landscape, American Impressionism, 20th-century realism and abstraction, New Deal projects, sculpture, photography,
prints and drawings, African American art, Latino art,
and folk art are featured in the collection. Contemporary American crafts are featured at the Smithsonian
American Art Museum's Renwick Gallery (see p. 195).

Two early Puerto Rican wood sculptures, *Santa
Barbara* from about 1680 to 1690 and *Nuestra Señora
de los Dolores (Our Lady of Sorrows)* from about 1675
to 1725, are the oldest works in the collection. Colonial
America is represented with portraits by John Singleton Copley, Charles Willson Peale, and Gilbert Stuart,
landscapes by Thomas Cole, and sculptures by Horatio
Greenough.

The nation's first American art collection comprises more than 300 years of painting, sculpture, folk art, photography, and graphic art. The museum's historic Greek Revival building in the heart of the nation's capital has been meticulously renovated with expanded permanent collection galleries and the new Luce Foundation Center for American Art, the first visible art storage and study center in Washington. A wide array of free public programs are offered; visit AmericanArt.si.edu for information.

For decades, the museum championed the artists who captured the spirit of the frontier and the lure of the West. George Catlin, Frederic Remington, Thomas Moran, and Albert Bierstadt celebrated the landscape and paid tribute to Native Americans and their cultures.

The museum has one of the finest and largest collections of American Impressionist paintings and artwork from the last quarter of the 19th century, a period dubbed the "Gilded Age" by author Mark Twain. Artists included are Childe Hassam, Mary Cassatt, William Merritt Chase, Winslow Homer, John Singer Sargent, and James McNeill Whistler.

The country's largest collection of New Deal art and murals can also be found at the Smithsonian American Art Museum. Realist painters include Edward Hopper, John Sloan, and Andrew Wyeth.

Some American modernists, like Georgia O'Keeffe and Joseph Stella, captured the spirit of their age with inventive new ways of depicting the world, while artists such as Willem de Kooning and Franz Kline created wholly abstract compositions. Other important 20th-century painters in the collection are Marsden Hartley, Stuart Davis, Wayne Thiebaud, Alfred Jensen, and Philip Guston.

In recent years, the museum has focused on acquiring major works by modern and contemporary artists, including Oscar Bluemner, Christo, Nancy Graves, David Hockney, Jenny Holzer, Edward and Nancy Kienholz, Liz Larner, Roy Lichtenstein, Nam June Paik, Martin Puryear, and James Rosenquist.

The museum's sculpture collection, ranging from works by 19th-century masters Horatio Greenough, Edmonia Lewis, Harriet Hosmer, and Augustus Saint-Gaudens to renowned 20th-century artists Louise Nevelson, Isamu Noguchi, and Edward Kienholz, is the largest collection of American sculpture anywhere. Works on paper comprise a large part of the collection, notably prints from the 20th century and more than 150 years of photography.

The Smithsonian American Art Museum also has a long tradition of championing works that initially did not have a place in the story of American art. The museum was one of the first museums to collect and display folk art in its galleries. In the last decade, it has acquired almost 500 pieces of Latino art, spanning colonial times to today.

Extensive holdings by William H. Johnson are part of the museum's notable collection of more than 2,000 artworks by African American artists. Other African American artists represented include Robert Scott Duncanson, Henry Ossawa Tanner, Horace Pippin, Romare Bearden, Jacob Lawrence, Louis Mailou Jones, and Sam Gilliam.

James Rosenquist (b. 1933), *Industrial Cottage*, 1977, oil on canvas. © 1977 James Rosenquist.

GENERAL INFORMATION
(For Portrait Gallery and American Art)

BUILDING HISTORY

The Smithsonian American Art Museum and the National Portrait Gallery share a National Historic Landmark building located in the heart of Washington, DC's vibrant downtown. A recent renovation (2000-2006) has restored exceptional architectural features, such as porticos modeled on the Parthenon, a graceful curving double staircase, colonnades, vaulted galleries illuminated by natural light and skylights as long as a city block.

Modern enhancements, such as the Lunder Conservation Center and the Kogod Courtyard, honor the forward-thinking ideas and American ingenuity that have always been celebrated in the building from its early days as the nation's Patent Office. The building is now a dazzling showcase for art and portraiture that celebrates the vision and creativity of Americans.

Begun in 1836 and completed in 1868, the Patent Office Building is one of the oldest public buildings constructed in early Washington. Several important early American architects were involved in the original design of the building, preeminently Robert Mills (1781–1855). It is considered one of the finest examples of Greek Revival architecture in the United States.

Patent models, the government's historical, scientific, and art collections, including the Declaration of Independence and George Washington's Revolutionary War camp tent, were displayed on the third floor. During the Civil War, the building was used as a temporary military hospital and barracks. In March 1865, it was the site of President Abraham Lincoln's inaugural ball.

In the 1950s, the building was scheduled for demolition, but the nascent historic preservation movement successfully campaigned to save it. Congress transferred the building to the Smithsonian in 1958, and the museums opened to the public in the building in 1968.

INFORMATION DESK
Located in the lobby

TOURS
Walk-in tours with museum docents are offered. For information on group tours please call 202-633-1000.

PUBLIC PROGRAMS
Free public programs include gallery talks, films, illustrated lectures, artist workshops, family days, and performances of music, dance, and theater. For information call 202-633-1000 or visit AmericanArt.si.edu and npg.si.edu.

MEMBERSHIP
Become a member and join two museums for the price of one. The Smithsonian American Art Museum and the National Portrait Gallery connect you to America's stories through art, history, and biography. For more information, call the membership office at 202-633-6362 or visit AmericanArt.si.edu and npg.si.edu.

MUSEUM STORE
The museum stores on the first floor feature collection-inspired gifts, note cards, posters, books, calendars, jewelry, and more.

CAFÉ
The Courtyard Café offers casual dining with a seasonal menu of American-inspired dishes. It is open from 11:30 A.M. to 4 P.M.; coffee, beer and wine, and light-fare are available until 6:30 P.M.

WI-FI
Free public wireless Internet access (Wi-Fi) is available in the Kogod Courtyard and the Luce Foundation Center for American Art.

Opposite: Luce Foundation Center for American Art. Below: Robert and Arlene Kogod Courtyard.

Above: Albert Paley (b. 1944), Portal Gates, 1974, forged steel, brass, copper, and bronze. Opposite top: Dale Chihuly, (b. 1941) *Cobalt and Gold Leaf Venetian*, 1993, blown glass with surface ornamentation. Opposite bottom: Renwick Gallery of the Smithsonian American Art Museum

Pennsylvania Avenue at
17th Street, NW
Open daily from
10 A.M. to 5:30 P.M.
Closed December 25.
Metrorail: Farragut
West station
(17th Street exit).
Museum information:
(recorded)
202-633-7970.
Smithsonian
information:
202-633-1000.
TTY: 202-633-5285.
www.AmericanArt.si.edu

RENWICK GALLERY OF THE SMITHSONIAN AMERICAN ART MUSEUM

The Renwick Gallery, a branch of the Smithsonian American Art Museum, is dedicated to exhibiting American crafts and decorative arts from the 19th century to the present. The building, named in honor of its architect, James Renwick, Jr., has been home to the museum's contemporary craft program since 1972.

The permanent collection galleries on the second floor showcase works of art in clay, fiber, glass, metal, wood, and mixed media. Artists represented in the Renwick Gallery collection include Anni Albers, Wendell Castle, John Cederquist, Dale Chihuly, Larry Fuente, Kim Schmahman, Harvey Littleton, Albert Paley, Peter Voulkos, and Betty Woodman.

The extraordinary Grand Salon, a 4,300-square-foot gallery with a soaring 40-foot ceiling, is considered one of Washington's premier spaces. It features

AT A GLANCE

Changing exhibitions of American crafts and decorative arts—historic and contemporary as well as selections from the permanent collection of 20th- and 21st-century American crafts—are on view in this distinguished building. The Grand Salon recreates the elegant setting of a 19th-century collector's picture gallery.

paintings from the museum's collection hung salon-style, top-to-bottom and side-by-side, creating the elegant setting of a 19th century collector's picture gallery.

Over more than three decades, the Renwick Gallery has presented groundbreaking exhibitions devoted to modern craft traditions. Special exhibitions, presented

in the spring and fall, address major issues in American crafts and decorative arts such as sources, influences, and historical traditions.

BUILDING HISTORY

The Renwick Gallery building was begun in 1859 to house the art collection of William Wilson Corcoran, a prominent Washington philanthropist and banker. Corcoran engaged the noted architect James Renwick Jr., who had earlier designed the Smithsonian's Castle and St. Patrick's Cathedral in New York City. Renwick modeled the gallery in the French Second-Empire style that was popular at the time.

Completed in 1861, it was the city's first art museum. Shortly thereafter, the Quarter Master General's Corps for the Union Army occupied the building for the duration of the Civil War. The building was returned to Corcoran in 1869. After extensive renovations, it finally opened as an art gallery in 1874.

Opposite: Larry Fuente (b. 1947), *Game Fish*, 1988. © 1988 Larry Fuente.

Below: Beth Lipman, (b. 1971) *Bancketje (Banquet)*, 2003, hand-sculpted, blown, kiln-formed and lamp-worked glass with gold paint, oak, oil, and mixed media.

Above: Peter Voulkos, (1924-2002), *Rocking Pot*, 1956, wheel-thrown and slab-constructed stoneware with colemanite wash. Opposite: Sam Maloof (1916-2009), *Double Rocking Chair*, 1992, fiddleback maple and ebony. © 1992 Sam Maloof F.A.C.C.

By 1897, Corcoran's collection had outgrown the building. The U.S. Court of Claims took over the building in 1899. In need of larger space by the 1950s, the Court of Claims proposed that the historic building be torn down. First Lady Jacqueline Kennedy led the effort to save this architectural and historical gem, and in 1965, S. Dillon Ripley, then secretary of the Smithsonian, met with President Lyndon Johnson to request that the gallery be turned over to the Smithsonian. The Renwick was subsequently dedicated "for use as a gallery of art, crafts and design." After an extensive renovation, the building reopened in 1972 as the home of the Smithsonian American Art Museum's contemporary craft program.

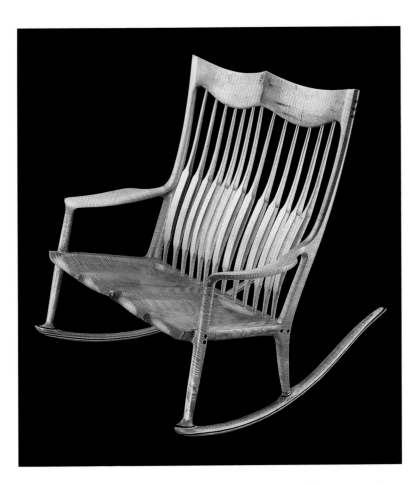

GENERAL INFORMATION

INFORMATION DESK

In the lobby

TOURS

Walk-in tours with museum docents are
offered. Group tours must be arranged
in advance by calling 202-633-8550.

PUBLIC PROGRAMS

Free public programs include craft
demonstrations, gallery talks, films,
and illustrated lectures. For information,
call 202-633-1000, or 202-633-5285
(TTY), or visit AmericanArt.si.edu.

MUSEUM STORE

The museum store features Renwick
pub-lications and other craft and decorative art books, craft objects
relating to exhibitions, postcards,
note cards, holiday cards, posters,
calendars, and jewelry.

MEMBERSHIP

Become a member of the Smithsonian
American Art Museum and enjoy special
benefits including a discount in Smithsonian stores. For more information,
call the membership office at 202-
633-6362 or visit AmericanArt.si.edu.

Above: Quilt, silk with embroidery, attributed to Kissie Gray, Saluda River, South Carolina, ca. 1855. Opposite above: Folk art piece *Equal* by Missionary Mary L. Proctor. Opposite below: Anacostia Community Museum after completion of a major renovation in 2001.

1901 Fort Place, SE.
Open daily from
10 A.M. to 5 P.M.
Closed December 25.
Metrorail:
Anacostia station.
Smithsonian
information:
202-633-4820
TTY: 202-633-5285.
www.anacostia.si.edu

ANACOSTIA
COMMUNITY MUSEUM

The Anacostia Community Museum documents and interprets the effect of historical and contemporary social and cultural issues on communities. The museum has emerged as an innovator in developing exhibits and programs that challenge perceptions, generate new knowledge, and deepen understanding about the ever-changing concepts and realities of "community." Formerly focused solely on African American heritage, the museum has used that experience and the issues confronting the Anacostia community in which it was founded to expand from "legacy" themes and issues based on ethnicity to broader cultural issues that resonate within communities worldwide.

A major renovation of the building in 2001 reorganized the physical plant and expanded library and collections-care

AT A GLANCE

The Anacostia Community Museum was established in 1967 as the nation's first federally funded neighborhood museum. The museum became a significant national and community-oriented resource based on its earlier focus on African American history and culture. Drawing on that expertise, its research, exhibitions, and public program activities now explore the realities and permutations of community locally and internationally.

facilities. These improvements have enabled the museum to broaden its efforts to collect and preserve artifacts that support its expanded mission as well as augment its legacy collection and revolving exhibition program.

Scholars and researchers continue to find unique opportunities to use the excellent research facilities at the Anacostia Community Museum. The museum's collections of archival materials, photographs, books, and artifacts reflect neighborhood and city history, women's history, literature, family history, and African American studies. A major research thrust is the Community Documentation Center which records the history and changes in the museum's surrounding communities and is the basis for broader national and international issues addressed in exhibitions and programs under the museum's expanded direction.

Research, collection development, and outreach at the museum are models for replication by other community-oriented museums. An active publications program features education and exhibition-related materials and publications on local, national,

and international community related issues. *The Black Washingtonians: The Anacostia Museum Illustrated Chronology* was published in 2005; several books are forthcoming on the built environment, churches and church archives, and urban rivers.

GENERAL INFORMATION

HOW TO GET THERE

The Anacostia Museum is located in historic Fort Stanton Park in southeast Washington, DC, with ample parking for cars and buses.

By Metrorail and Metrobus: Take the Green Line to the Anacostia station and transfer to the W-2 or W-3 Metrobus to the museum. *By car:* From downtown, take the southeast Freeway (I-395) to the 11th Street Bridge and exit at Martin Luther King Jr. Avenue. At the fourth traffic light, turn left at Morris Road and drive up the hill to the museum. *From I-295 south:* Take the Howard Road exit and turn left on Howard Road. Travel to Martin Luther King Jr. Avenue and turn left. Turn right at Morris Road and continue up the hill to the museum.

INFORMATION DESK

In the entrance lobby.

SPECIAL ACTIVITIES AND TOURS

Special activities for adults and children include lectures, workshops, films, and performances. A calendar of events is available on request. For information about exhibitions and programs, call 202-633-4844. To schedule a tour, call the Education Department at 202-633-4844. Visit the museum's Web site at anacostia.si.edu.

RESEARCH

The museum's Research Department provides fellowship and internship opportunities to undergraduate and graduate students in public history, community-oriented studies, and African American studies. Internships are also available in the Collections, Design and Production, Education, Special Events, and Public Affairs departments. For more information about internships call 202-633-4820/202-633-4826, or email gualitieria@si.edu.

Above: This airplane was constructed by folk artist Leslie Payne as part of an installation, complete with an airfield and runway, an air tower, and a machine shop. Opposite: "East of the River: Continuity and Change" (2007) reviewed the history and development of the communities east of the Anacostia River for the past 200 years.

Above: The Zoo's male giant panda rests in his habitat. Opposite top: The National Zoo is working to save the Bali mynah from extinction. Opposite bottom: The Zoo's main pedestrian entrance is located on Connecticut Avenue.

NATIONAL ZOOLOGICAL PARK

Entrances: Connecticut Avenue, NW (3001 block between Cathedral Avenue and Devonshire Place); Harvard Street and Adams Mill Road intersection; Beach Drive in Rock Creek Park. Open daily. See page 215 for hours. Closed December 25. Metrorail: Woodley Park/Zoo/ Adams Morgan station or Cleveland Park station. Recorded information: 202-633-4800. Information Desk: 202-633-4888. National Zoo: nationalzoo.si.edu

The National Zoo is known internationally for the display, breeding, and study of wild animals. Most of the Zoo's animals live in naturalistic settings that comfortably house social groups resembling those found in the wild.

Vertebrate species, representing the most spectacular and familiar forms of land animals, make up the most visible part of the collection, but invertebrate and aquatic species provide a more comprehensive picture of animal life. Educational graphics, learning carts, and family-oriented learning labs (including "How Do You Zoo?" in the Visitor Center and the Bird Resource Center in the Bird House) supplement public understanding of the park's animals and plants.

Native and ornamental plants grow throughout the 163-acre park. The Native

Above: The National Zoo's giant pandas enjoy their habitat. Opposite: Flamingos are a summer staple at the National Zoo.

American Heritage Garden, African American Heritage Garden, and butterfly garden (featuring plants that attract butterflies) provide living examples of the interaction among plants, animals, and humans. Olmsted Walk, the central path, connects the major animal exhibits. It is named for the father of landscape architecture, Frederick Law Olmsted, who created the original design for the National Zoo as well as the U.S. Capitol grounds, the Washington National Cathedral grounds, and New York's Central Park.

EXHIBITS

The giant pandas occupy the top spot on the Zoo's "must-see" list. The pandas' state-of-the-art habitat is designed to mimic the pandas' natural habitat of rocky, lush terrain in China. Each element has a purpose—from helping the pandas stay cool in hot weather to giving them a place to hide when they need privacy. There are rock and tree structures perfect for climbing; grottoes, pools, and streams for keeping cool.

The pandas are the gateway to Asia Trail—nearly six acres of exhibits featuring endangered or threatened

Top: The world's largest lizard, the Komodo dragon, uses its tongue to explore its environment. Bottom: The brilliantly colored green tree pythons are a favorite in the Zoo's Reptile Discovery Center.

Asian species. Joining giant pandas along the Trail are clouded leopards, fishing cats, Asian small-clawed otters, red pandas, and sloth bears.

The approach to the Bird House leads visitors over Wetlands, a series of sheltered ponds surrounded by tall grasses and other vegetation. The exhibit showcases the diverse but little understood wetland ecosystem and the waterfowl and wading birds native to swampy areas. The Bird House, built in 1928, includes one of the zoo world's first great flight rooms, an indoor courtyard open to both birds and visitors. Exotic, jewel-toned birds fly and perch in its lush, tropical habitat. Other Bird House inhabitants include numerous endangered species, such as the Bali mynah, the Guam rail (extinct in the wild), and a variety of Hawaiian birds. Outdoor enclosures provide tranquil space for flamingos, assorted cranes, cassowaries, and Kori bustards.

Asian elephants are critically endangered; fewer than 45,000 remain in their native countries. The National Zoo is committed to their conservation and to the powerful connection made when visitors experience the magnificence of elephants in the Zoo.

The National Zoo's Asian elephant exhibit is undergoing expansion and transformation, using the original building completed in 1937 as the project's foundation. Elephant Trails will include indoor and outdoor habitats that stimulate the natural behaviors of a matriarchal herd of elephants—the ultimate goal for the Zoo's Asian elephant program.

Opening in 2011, Elephant Trails will include an indoor communal area that serves as the hub of the herd's social life. Outside habitats will provide activities and options—an exercise path, a waterfall or pool, sand piles or heavy forest—all managed by expert Zoo staff.

At the Reptile Discovery Center, families with school-age children can explore the biology of reptiles and amphibians. Visitors may use listening, visual, and olfactory skills to investigate how "herptiles" feed and communicate. Afterward, families can apply their knowledge to

living animals, which include alligator turtles, king cobras, tentacled snakes, alligators, gavials, and Komodo dragons. The Reptile Discovery Center is located in the former Reptile House. Fantastical carved reptiles, sculpted doors, and columns at its main entrance decorate the facade of this Romanesque building which, when it

opened in 1931, was recognized by the American Institute of Architects as the outstanding brick building in the eastern United States.

In the Invertebrate Exhibit, the diverse, but often ignored, world of animals without backbones comes to life. Insects, sponges, sea stars, mollusks, crabs, and other invertebrates—the creatures that make up the vast majority of living things—are stunningly exhib-

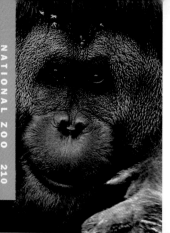

ited in ways that allow for close-up study. In an adjoining glass-enclosed addition, the Pollinarium's blooming plants, butterflies, and bees illustrate the evolution, the beauty, and the role of animals in plant reproduction.

Think Tank introduces visitors to the science of animal cognition. Thinking ability in animals is presented through the topics of tool use, language, and society. Orangutans, macaques, hermit crabs, leaf-cutter ants, as well as computers and games stimulate exploration. Orangutans can move between the Think Tank and their Great Ape House enclosures, several hundred feet farther along Olmsted Walk, by swinging, or brachiating, across the Orangutan Transport System. This series of towers connected by heavy cables allows orangutans to move as they would in their heavily forested, tropical homes.

Top: Several of the National Zoo's orangutans participate in a computer-based language project at Think Tank. Bottom: The National Zoo's gorilla family gives visitors insights into the great ape's behavior and social structure. Opposite: Sumatran tigers, extremely rare in the wild, are ambassadors for the Zoo's conservation and science initiatives.

Great Cats is home territory for some of the Zoo's favorite animals: lions and tigers. Other highlights of the exhibit include Tiger Tracks, a 250-foot-long educational trail lined with displays comparing life in a tiger family to family interactions among humans. The Predator's Alcove, a 500-square-foot museum-style display, showcases spectacular sharp-toothed fossils and explains the ecology of large carnivores.

A walk through Amazonia introduces visitors to the high degree of biological diversity in a tropical rainforest. The 15,000-square-foot rainforest habitat of the exhibit includes a cascading tropical river and a 55,000-gallon aquarium for the display of Amazon River fish. Within Amazonia's dome, visitors find a living tropical forest with more than 350 species of plants, including 50-foot-tall trees, tropical vines, and epiphytes. This habitat is also home to dozens of species of mammals, birds, reptiles, amphibians, and

insects typical of the Amazon Basin, all moving throughout the exhibit.

The "Amazonia Science Gallery" is an 8,000-square-foot experimental science education/outreach center that brings visitors into the day-to-day world of scientific research and the people who do it. The "Amazonia Science Gallery" includes Amphibian Alert!—a hands-on exhibit—featuring over 15 species of frogs and other amphibians, including the extinct-in-the-wild Panamanian Golden Frog. Through close-up animal views and interactive exhibits, visitors discover what's threatening these amphibian "jewels" and what's being done to save them. New to the Amazonia Science Gallery is Science On a Sphere (SOS)®, a state-of-the-art exhibit created by the National Oceanic and Atmospheric Administration. SOS® effectively illustrates Earth System science to people of all ages.

The Visitor Center, near the Connecticut Avenue entrance, has an auditorium, a bookstore, restrooms, and an interactive learning center. "How Do You Zoo?" (open Saturdays and Sundays from 10 A.M. to 4 P.M.) gives children between the ages of 5 and 10 the chance to role play as a zookeeper, veterinarian, or nutritionist.

The National Zoo's cheetah Conservation Station allows visitors to see this endangered cat in a naturalistic habitat that encourages behavior typical to that observed in the wild.

CONSERVATION AND RESEARCH

What the visitor sees at the National Zoo reveals only a small part of the Zoo's complexity as a scientific research organization. National Zoo scientists, working on the grounds in Washington, DC, and at the 3,200-acre Smithsonian Conservation Biology Institute in Front Royal, Virginia, were among the founders of the field of conservation biology. National Zoo scientists continue as leaders today, with global perspectives and

long-term experience in conducting zoo- and field-based research. Their discoveries enhance the survival or recovery of species and their habitats, helping to ensure the health and well-being of animals in zoos and their counterparts in the wild. The National Zoo is also a global leader in training the next generation of conservation and zoo professionals through undergraduate, graduate, and professional education that emphasizes well-founded approaches to conservation.

Above: A male Mexican wolf at the National Zoo is part of a Species Survival Plan. Below: The barks of sea lions attract visitors to the Zoo's Beaver Valley.

HISTORY

Although the Smithsonian Institution received gifts of live animals almost from its beginning, there was no zoo to house and study the living collection. Some of the animals were sent to zoos elsewhere; some were kept on the National Mall. Over the years, a sizable menagerie accumulated outside the Smithsonian Castle. In 1889, Congress established the National Zoological Park at the

The National Zoo is one of the few places outside New Zealand where people can observe a live kiwi. The Zoo has successfully bred these unique birds. Opposite: Orange julia butterflies can be seen in the Zoo's Pollinarium exhibit.

urging of Samuel Pierpont Langley, third Secretary of the Smithsonian, and William T. Hornaday, a Smithsonian naturalist who was particularly concerned about the looming extinction of the American bison. Six bison were among the animals transferred from the Mall to the National Zoo when the grounds opened in 1891.

Animal collecting expeditions in the early 1900s, together with gifts from individuals and foreign governments and exchanges with other zoos, augmented the Zoo's population and introduced Washingtonians to rare and exotic animals, including the Tasmanian wolf (now extinct), bongo, and Komodo dragon.

Today, the National Zoo continues to develop a bond between humans and animals that helps the public understand biology and scientific concepts that will guide them in making informed choices in daily life. Exhibits, educational programs, school programs, training opportunities, and public lectures all bring the rich diversity of life on Earth to a variety of local, national, and international audiences. In the 21st century, the Zoo's mission is to provide leadership in animal science, conservation, and public education.

FRIENDS OF THE NATIONAL ZOO

Friends of the National Zoo (FONZ) is a non-profit, membership-based organization dedicated to supporting the conservation, education, and science mission of the Smithsonian's National Zoo. Since 1958, FONZ has supported the Zoo by implementing education, membership, and volunteer programs, hosting special events, raising funds for Zoo projects, providing guest services for Zoo visitors, and grants to Zoo scientists.

To learn more about FONZ programs and membership options, see www.fonz.org.

GENERAL INFORMATION

HOW TO GET THERE

The Zoo is accessible from the Woodley Park/Zoo/Adams Morgan and Cleveland Park Metrorail stations and is accessible by Metrobus. For Metro information, call 202-637-7000, or 202-638-3780 (TTY), or check the Web site www.wmata.com. Limited pay parking is available on Zoo lots. Bus-passenger discharge and pickup and limited free bus parking are available.

HOURS (unless otherwise posted)

April–October: Animal exhibits are open from 10 A.M. to 6 P.M. every day. November–March: Animal exhibits are open from 10 A.M. to 5 P.M. every day. The Zoo is open every day except December 25.

TOURS

Guided weekend highlight tours of the Zoo for families, individuals, or groups are available with an eight-week advance reservation. Call Friends of the National Zoo at 202-633-3025.

SERVICES

The Zoo has ramped building entrances and restroom facilities for nonambulatory visitors. Strollers may be rented in season for a small fee. A limited number of wheelchairs are available to borrow. Zoo police provide lost-and-found service and a refuge for lost children.

WHERE TO EAT

The Zoo has a variety of fast-food facilities. Picnic areas are located throughout the grounds, but no outdoor cooking is permitted.

GIFT SHOPS AND BOOKSTORE

Unique zoo-oriented souvenirs, postcards, books, T-shirts, and art objects are for sale.

FEEDING TIMES

Check at the information desks for feeding times and demonstrations.

HELPFUL HINTS

Consider using public transportation. Zoo parking lots often fill up early in the warm months. Wear comfortable  clothing and shoes. During the warmer months, visit early in the day or in the evening, when the park is less crowded and the animals are more active. Fall and early winter are great times to visit the Zoo. For more information, visit nationalzoo.si.edu.

SOME RULES TO FOLLOW

Pets, except certified assistance animals, are not permitted in the park. The area between the guardrail and the enclosure barrier is for your safety and that of the animals. Stay on your side of the guardrail. Zoo animals are wild and easily excited. Do not feed or attempt to touch the animals. The Zoo provides excellent, balanced diets, and additional feeding is unhealthy for them. Do not skate or ride bicycles in the park. Radios and other audio devices must be used with earphones.

Above: Wallpaper, René Crevel (French), ca. 1920. Opposite top: "Atomic" clock, George Nelson Associates, 1949. Opposite bottom: Back view of Cooper-Hewitt, National Design Museum.

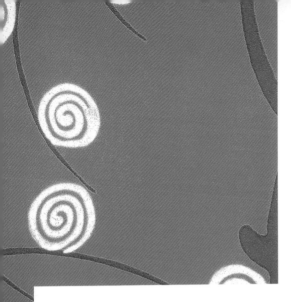

2 East 91st Street
(at Fifth Avenue),
New York City.
Open Monday
through Friday, 10 A.M.
to 5 P.M.; Saturday,
10 A.M. to 6 P.M.;
Sunday 12 P.M. to 6 P.M.
Closed January 1,
Thanksgiving,
December 25.
Admission charged.
Information:
212-849-8400.
cooperhewitt.org

COOPER-HEWITT, NATIONAL DESIGN MUSEUM

Cooper-Hewitt, National Design Museum is the only museum in the nation devoted exclusively to historic and contemporary design. The museum embraces fields as varied as architecture; industrial, landscape, interior, and graphic design; textiles; and fashion. With the conviction that design touches everyone, every day, in the spaces in which they live and work, the objects they use, and the messages they read and send, the museum presents compelling perspectives on the impact of design through dynamic exhibitions, educational programs, and publications.

Cooper-Hewitt was founded in 1897 by Amy, Eleanor, and Sarah Hewitt—granddaughters of industrialist Peter Cooper. A branch of the Smithsonian since 1967, the museum is housed in the magnificent Andrew Carnegie mansion on Fifth Avenue in New York City.

EXHIBITIONS

Cooper-Hewitt's galleries are devoted to changing exhibitions that examine the impact of design on daily life, exploring the interplay of aesthetics, commerce, and technology. Ranging from thematic, collections-based presentations of historic design to installations by contemporary architects and industrial designers, Cooper-Hewitt's exhibitions exemplify the breadth and diversity of its historic collections as well as the latest in international design.

NANCY AND EDWIN MARKS GALLERY

In the renovated Music Room of the Carnegie Mansion, Cooper-Hewitt presents a rotating series of exhibitions drawn from the Museum's vast permanent collections. In addition to displays conceived by curatorial staff, Cooper-Hewitt engages guest interpreters, including artists, journalists, authors, and designers, to explore the collections and develop a personal thesis supported by a selection of objects from the Museum's collection. Guest curators have included Nigerian-British artist Yinka Shonibare, Dutch designer Hella Jongerius, writer and radio host Kurt Andersen, and Pakistani-born artist Shazia Sikander.

SOLOS SERIES

The *Solos* series was developed in 2003 to showcase innovations in the fields of architecture and design by examining a singular work, designer, or theme. Past *Solos* exhibitions include the architectural prototype FutureShack, designed to provide low-cost housing for refugees and the

Barcelona chair, model #90, Ludwig Mies van der Rohe (German), 1929.

homeless by re-appropriating existing materials; an
installation by celebrated French industrial designer
Matali Crasset; and *Tulou*, Chinese architectural firm
Urbanus's for affordable housing in China.

**Treasures from the
Collection, 2003.**

NATIONAL DESIGN TRIENNIAL

Launched to critical acclaim in 2000, the *Triennial*
presents architecture; interior, product, and graphic
design; and new media from around the world that
demonstrate the impulses, issues, and ideas driving
contemporary design. The only exhibition of its kind
in the country, the *Triennial* features the work of
approximately 85 designers, focusing on emerging
talent as well as a selection of mature leaders.

COLLECTIONS

With more than 200,000 objects spanning more
than 2,000 years, Cooper-Hewitt is one of the
largest repositories of design in the world. Its
collections are international in scope and date

Top: Furnishing fabric, produced by Favre, France, early 19th century. Bottom: Matchsafe with tinder cord, Russia, late 19th century. Opposite top: *Feathers*, Alexander Girard (American), 1957. Opposite bottom: Chair, Charles Eames (American), 1944.

from China's Han dynasty to the present. It has impressive holdings of furniture, metalwork, glass, ceramics, jewelry, woodwork, embroidery, woven and printed textiles, lace, and wallcoverings. The museum also has one of the largest collections of drawings in the United States, a large collection of prints—including examples of architectural drawings, advertising, and fashion, theater, and interior design—and the National Design Library. The collections are organized in four curatorial departments—Product Design and Decorative Arts; Drawings, Prints, and Graphic Design; Textiles; and Wallcoverings—and are supported by design archives and a reference library with more than 70,000 volumes, including 5,000 rare books.

INFORMATION DESK
Just inside the main entrance

TOURS
Guided tours are available for groups of six or more by advance arrangement; call 212-849-8351. Free daily tours are scheduled for current exhibitions.

MUSEUM STORE
The Shop at Cooper-Hewitt, located near the main entrance, offers exhibition catalogues; postcards; books on the decorative arts, architecture, and design; books relating to the museum's collections; jewelry; ceramics; and gift items.

CAFÉ
The café—in the Agnes Bourne Bridge Gallery and Lester and Enid Morse Garden Room year-round, and extending into the Arthur Ross Terrace and Garden in warm-weather months—serves a full selection of sandwiches, pastries, chips, cold beverages, and tea and coffee.

EDUCATIONAL PROGRAMS
The museum has an active calendar of workshops, courses, lectures, study tours, and seminars throughout the year, including programs for all ages and the entire family. Special children's programs are available for school groups. With Parsons the New School for Design, Cooper-Hewitt offers a two-year program leading to a master of arts degree in the history of decorative arts.

RESEARCH FACILITIES
The National Design Library contains more than 70,000 volumes, including 5,000 rare books. The library's picture collections include material on color, pattern, textiles, symbols, advertising, and interior and industrial design. It also has graphic and industrial design archives.

Above: Silver flatware,
George Washington
Maher (American), 1912.
Opposite: *Ladies' Old
Fashioned Shoes,*
Plate IX, T. Watson
Greig, Edinburgh,
Scotland, 1885.

SMITHSONIAN ACROSS AMERICA

The Smithsonian's commitment to reach Americans beyond Washington, DC, has never been stronger. New collaborations are taking shape between the Smithsonian and museums, cultural and educational organizations, and communities across the nation. The Smithsonian's National Programs offer a variety of traveling exhibits, educational workshops, cultural presentations, and partnership opportunities, all of which can be tailored and combined to meet the needs of organizations and communities across America. Visit the Smithsonian Across America Web site, saa.si.edu to view a calendar of Smithsonian exhibitions and programs taking place in your state. Four Smithsonian units work together to achieve this national outreach mission; they are described on the following pages.

THE SMITHSONIAN ASSOCIATES

The Smithsonian Associates provides educational and cultural programs that highlight and complement the work of the Smithsonian Institution. Through a wide variety of programs offered on the National Mall, in the Washington Metro area, and across the country, the Smithsonian strengthens its connections with the public. The Smithsonian Associates is recognized as the nation's largest and most esteemed museum-based continuing education program.

Through its Resident Associate Program, Washington area audiences of all ages can enjoy a broad array of lectures, seminars, performing arts events, workshops, and local tours.

The "Scholars in the Schools" and "Voices of Discovery" programs take outstanding scholars from the Smithsonian's research and curatorial staff into schools, museums, libraries, senior citizen and youth groups, and civic organizations to conduct inspiring presentations. Additional programs offered through The Smithsonian Associates include the Master of Arts Degree in the History of Decorative Arts, a collaborative effort with the distinguished Corcoran College of Art + Design; the Art Collectors Program, a series of commissioned, limited-edition artwork available for purchase; and the Young Benefactors, a fundraising cultural membership organization. For more information about The Smithsonian Associates program call 202-633-3030 or visit www.SmithsonianAssociates.org.

The Smithsonian Associates' Resident Associate Program brings noted scholars, authors, politicians, and cultural icons to Washington area audiences. In 2008, actress Meryl Streep was presented with the Benjamin Franklin Creativity Laureate Award in a special Smithsonian Associates program. Preceding pages: The 2008-2009 season of Discovery Theater celebrated the Year of the Puppet, in partnership with The Jim Henson Legacy and the SITES exhibition, "Jim Henson's Fantastic World." Photo courtesy of The Jim Henson Company. Kermit the Frog © The Muppets Studio, LLC.

SMITHSONIAN AFFILIATIONS

Smithsonian Affiliations is a major outreach effort designed to share the Smithsonian's collections with the American people through partnerships with museums, science centers, and cultural institutions across the country. Affiliations are long-term relationships between partnering organizations and the Smithsonian Institution; artifacts from the national collections are

loaned for a period of up to ten years, allowing numerous opportunities for exhibitions, educational programs, and national collaborations. Smithsonian Affiliations also creates internship and fellowship opportunities for students and museum staff across the country, provides technical support and training, and assists affiliate organizations through collaborative marketing and membership programs. For more information regarding Smithsonian Affiliations call 202-633-5300 or visit www.affiliations.si.edu.

Visitors at the San Diego Air & Space Museum, a Smithsonian Affiliate, view the Apollo 9 space capsule, on loan from the Smithsonian's National Air and Space Museum.

SMITHSONIAN CENTER FOR EDUCATION AND MUSEUM STUDIES

The Smithsonian Center for Education and Museum Studies links the Smithsonian's educational resources and expertise to the nation's classrooms. It is the central education office of the Institution, providing leadership in museum-based education, strategic

**Students create
an exhibit using
Smithsonian-based
learning techniques.**

planning, and assessment. It produces and delivers Smithsonian educational experiences, services, and products informed by education research and Smithsonian expertise and collections, with particular emphasis on the needs of educators, families, and students. The center produces www.SmithsonianEducation.org, the gateway to all of the Institution's educational resources, and publishes *Smithsonian in Your Classroom,* a journal for schools. For more information call 202-633-5330 or visit www.SmithsonianEducation.org.

THE SMITHSONIAN INSTITUTION TRAVELING EXHIBITION SERVICE

The Smithsonian Institution Traveling Exhibition Service (SITES) has been sharing the wealth of Smithsonian collections and research programs with millions of people outside Washington, DC, for more than 50 years. SITES connects Americans to their shared cultural heritage through a wide range of exhibitions about art, science, and history. Exhibitions are shown not only in museums but wherever people live, work, and play: in libraries, science centers, historical societies, community centers, botanical gardens, schools, and shopping malls. Exhibition descriptions and tour schedules are available on the Web. For more information call 202-633-3168 or visit www.sites.si.edu.

The Smithsonian Institution Traveling Exhibition Service brings engaging exhibits to hundreds of cities and towns across the country. *Dig It! The Secrets of Soil*, from the National Museum of Natural History, will begin its national tour in spring 2010.

SMITHSONIAN INSTITUTION MEMBERSHIPS

The Smithsonian invites people of all ages across the country and around the world to become Associate members. You may choose from an exciting array of membership programs. The benefits of each membership program are described below.

NATIONAL ASSOCIATE MEMBERSHIP

For members nationwide and worldwide, open to all.

SMITHSONIAN MAGAZINE (12 ISSUES). Illuminates an exciting world of the arts, sciences, history, and travel.

MEMBERS ONLY TRAVEL Eligibility for Smithsonian travel programs across the country and around the world with Smithsonian Journeys

AMENITIES IN WASHINGTON, DC A cordial welcome and special information materials at the museum information desks

SMITHSONIAN REGIONAL EVENTS. Invitations to special events occurring in your metropolitan area

FREE ADMISSION No charge for members visiting the Smithsonian's Cooper-Hewitt, National Design Museum in New York City

DISCOUNTS at Smithsonian Museum Stores (excluding the National Zoo and the separately administered National Gallery of Art), online at www.SmithsonianStore.com, and with Smithsonian Catalogue.

- 10 percent off meal purchases at select Smithsonian dining facilities, and reduced rates on tickets to the Smithsonian's IMAX® theaters and planetarium
- Special reduced member rates on Smithsonian Folkways Recordings purchased at www.folkways.si.edu and on limited-edition art through the Smithsonian Associates Art Collectors Program.

For more information, call 1-800-766-2149 or visit www.smithsonian.com.

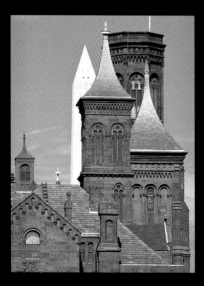

RESIDENT ASSOCIATE MEMBERSHIP

For Washington metropolitan-area residents, membership includes all National Associate benefits (excluding Smithsonian magazine at some levels), plus:

ASSOCIATE, a monthly catalog with details about more than 100 current programs and events

FREE lectures, tours, and family programs

DISCOUNTS, as much as 25 percent, on courses, workshops, lectures, films,

The rich spectacle of Kunqu, traditional Chinese musical drama combining elements of theater, opera, poetry, and music, presented by the Resident Associate Program.

seminars, performing arts events, and many more activities; an additional 10 percent for all members age 60 and over. **FREE PARKING** at the National Museum of Natural History when attending Resident Associate evening or weekend events (on a space-available basis; Resident Associate Program ticket required). **OPPORTUNITIES** for volunteer service

For more information, call 202-357-3030, or visit www.residentassociates.org.

FRIENDS OF THE SMITHSONIAN (FORMERLY CONTRIBUTING MEMBERSHIP & JAMES SMITHSON SOCIETY)

Those who join The Friends of the Smithsonian (formerly Contributing Membership and the James Smithson Society), its highest membership group, help shape the Smithsonian's collection, preservation, education, and research efforts through their generous philanthropic support. While all members receive National Associate benefits, additional exclusive benefits commensurate with each member level are also awarded, including:

GIFT EDITIONS of current Smithsonian books and recordings; the exquisite annual Smithsonian desk calendar and guidebook; and the Smithsonian's annual report;

RECEPTIONS AND BEHIND-THE-SCENES TOURS of the newest exhibitions and venues;

DEEP DISCOUNTS at Smithsonian stores, selected Smithsonian dining facilities, Smithsonian IMAX® theaters, Smithsonian catalog purchases, and on Folkways recordings.

Opposite: The Smithsonian Castle, in the heart of the nation's capital.

JAMES SMITHSON SOCIETY members enjoy exclusive receptions, behind-the-scenes tours, the *Food for Thought* summer luncheon series, and, each spring, the Members Weekend, including a formal Members' Dinner. **CHARITABLE-GIFT TAX DEDUCTIONS BASED ON LEVEL OF MEMBERSHIP.** For more information, call 1-800-931-3226 or e-mail membership@si.edu.

AIR & SPACE ASSOCIATE MEMBERSHIP

For enthusiasts of aviation, space flight, and modern technology. Membership includes the following benefits:

AIR & SPACE/SMITHSONIAN MAGAZINE (6 ISSUES). Chronicles and celebrates human conquest of the air and exploration of the Universe

MEMBERS-ONLY TRAVEL Eligibility for Smithsonian travel programs across the country and around the world with Smithsonian Journeys

AMENITIES IN WASHINGTON, DC. A cordial welcome and special information materials at the museum information desks

One of 12 lunar modules built for Project Apollo, "LM2" in the National Air and Space Museum was used for drop tests in Earth's atmosphere.

SMITHSONIAN REGIONAL EVENTS. Invitations to special events occurring in your metropolitan area.

DISCOUNTS at Smithsonian Museum Stores (excluding the National Zoo and the separately administered National Gallery of Art), online at www.SmithsonianStore.com, and with Smithsonian Catalogue.

- 10 percent off meal purchases at select Smithsonian dining facilities and reduced rates on tickets to the Smithsonian's IMAX® theaters and planetarium

For more information, call 1-800-766-2149 or visit www.airspacemag.com.

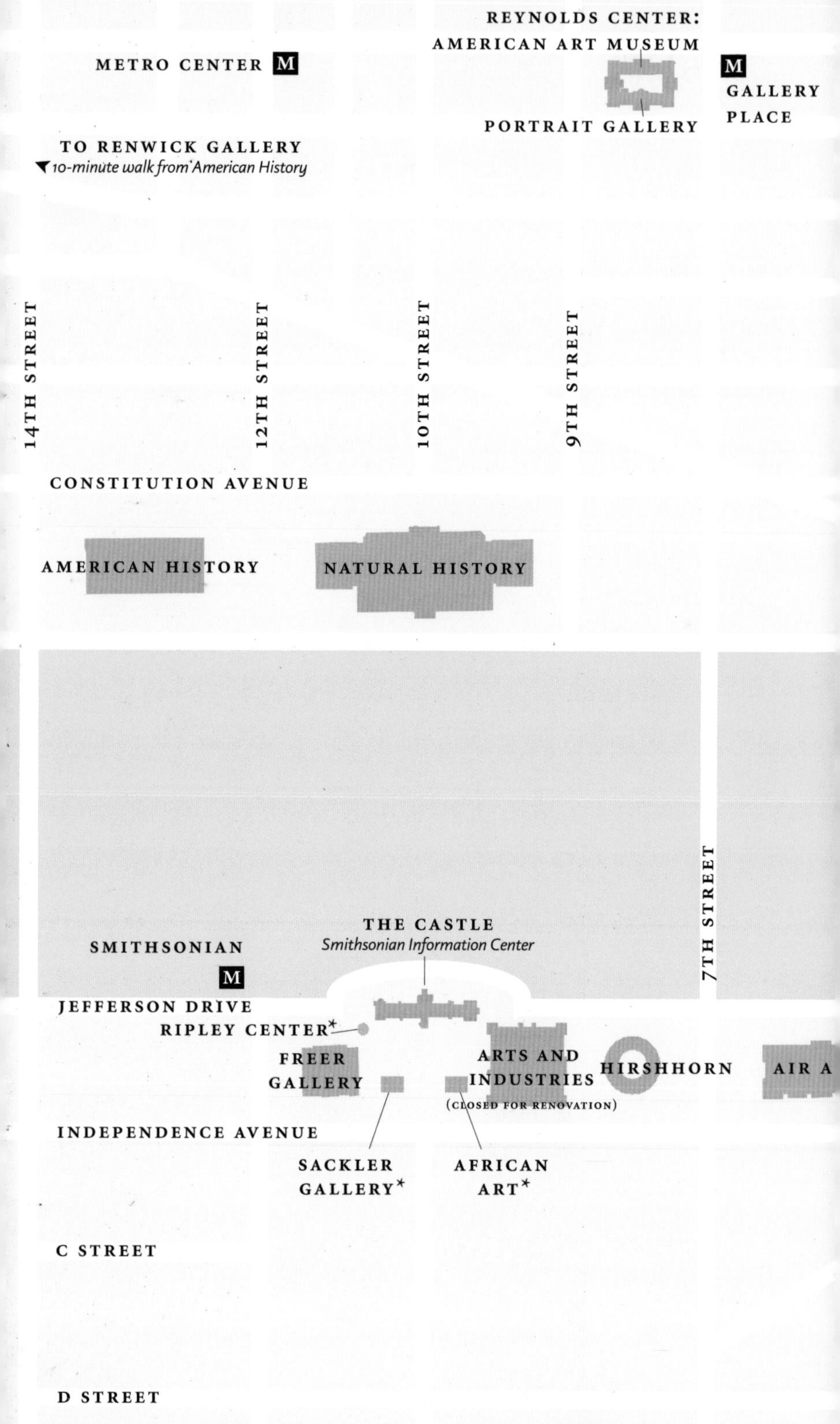

METRO CENTER **M**

REYNOLDS CENTER:
AMERICAN ART MUSEUM

M GALLERY PLACE

PORTRAIT GALLERY

TO RENWICK GALLERY
▼ *10-minute walk from American History*

14TH STREET

12TH STREET

10TH STREET

9TH STREET

CONSTITUTION AVENUE

AMERICAN HISTORY

NATURAL HISTORY

7TH STREET

SMITHSONIAN
M

THE CASTLE
Smithsonian Information Center

JEFFERSON DRIVE
RIPLEY CENTER *

FREER GALLERY

ARTS AND INDUSTRIES
(CLOSED FOR RENOVATION)

HIRSHHORN

AIR A

INDEPENDENCE AVENUE

SACKLER GALLERY *

AFRICAN ART *

C STREET

D STREET

An asterisk * *indicates an entrance pavilion to an underground building. The symbol* **M** *indicates a Metrorail station.*